The Barefoot Fisherman

Guide to the Emerald Coast

From Gulf Shores, Alabama, to Apalachicola, Florida

The Barefoot Fisherman
Guide to the Emerald Coast

From Gulf Shores, Alabama, to Apalachicola, Florida

Gregory Dew

CRANE HILL
PUBLISHERS

Copyright © 1999 by Gregory Dew
Illustrations: Palomar Knot and Blood Knot by Grant Tatum, courtesy Menasha Ridge Press
          Fish species by Ralph Havard with the exception of sailcat, southern stingray, and whiting
Maps: Scott Fuller
Design: Stacy Budge and Bob Weathers

Published by Crane Hill Publishers, www.cranehill.com
Printed in the United States of America

Library of Congress Cataloging-in-Publication Data
Dew, Gregory, 1973-
 The barefoot fisherman : guide to the emerald coast / by Gregory Dew.
p. cm.
 Includes index.
 ISBN 1-57587-093-2 (trade paper)
1. Saltwater fishing-Florida-Gulf Coast-Guidebooks.
2. Saltwater fishing-Alabama-Gulf Coast-Guidebooks. 3. Gulf
Coast (Fla.)-Guidebooks. 4. Gulf Coast (Ala.)-Guidebooks.
I. Title.
SH483.d49 1999
799.1'6634-dc21
99-17166

10   9   8   7   6   5   4   3   2   1

Dedicated to Grandpa Eddy and Dolores:
the trout and the woman that forever elude me.

TABLE OF CONTENTS

PREFACE

When I suggested to my publisher the idea of a Barefoot Fisherman's guide she passed it along to the production staff, who, in turn, made a mock-up cover for the promotions catalog.

"This guy walking on the beach is pretty and picturesque," I said to her, "but when I suggested 'barefoot' I was thinking more along the lines of kicking your boots off and popping the top on a cold one."

As in all things, fishing lends itself to a variety of interpretations. Whether you fish for sport, leisure, higher understanding, or just good fun is a matter of personal preference. At day's end, however, all interpretations merge into one fact: Even though you might call it a good day of fishing regardless of whether you catch anything, the finest moments are when the surface bubbles, the rod doubles over, and you engage with a siren sounding to the deep.

The Barefoot Fisherman caters to all anglers—novice and veteran—and is designed to be user friendly. For the beginner, the first chapter covers the saltwater basics, including what tackle to purchase, how to set up your rig, and how to use it all. Then come advanced fishing techniques, such as filleting, chumming, and gigging. Chapter 2 concludes the saltwater fishing lesson with the essentials for picking a prime location according to geography, tides, currents, winds, and water. The angler is now ready to tackle the best fishing holes on the Emerald Coast.

For fishermen old and new, Chapter 3 highlights the 40 hottest fishing spots between Gulf Shores, Alabama, and Apalachicola, Florida. Directions accompany these "Hot Spots," along with information about parking, boat access, and foot accessibility. Also discussed here are what baits to use, what species to expect, what times of year are best for which species, and where to find each species in a particular locale. Each Hot Spot is concluded with a chart listing species, baits, and seasons, providing quick reference for the fisherman on the fly.

Chapter 4 features an extensive list of Emerald Coast species, including illustrations, descriptions, and detailed techniques on how to angle them. Use this to identify catches and as a supplement to the angling tips noted in the quick-reference charts of each Hot Spot. The guide concludes with recipes and a list of local fishing links (addresses, telephone numbers, websites, etc.), thus providing everything necessary, and then some, for a great day of angling along the Emerald Coast.

The northern Gulf of Mexico is truly a fisherman's paradise. It is home to some of the most exceptional and diversified fishing in the world. Many of the Hot Spots and techniques featured in this book I stumbled across myself. Others were introduced to me by locals willing to share their secrets so that we all might enjoy fishing, as well as the things that go along with it. But that is fishing. It always returns to us whatever we are willing to give, and we always return to it, regardless of our reasoning or without reasoning at all.

ACKNOWLEDGMENTS

Thanks to the caretakers at Red Bar for keeping my priorities straight. To my family for keeping my dumpster diving to a minimum. To Sue and Rick for the use of Suite 200 and the cordless phone. To the many Madams at Crane Hill. To Isie, who I've been privy to know before, during, and after. To JC, who always knows better. To all those I've haphazardly forgotten who believe in working to live, and not the other way around. And a special thanks to the Holland family: loving wife and mother, 'B,' for reinforcing the need for the four basic food groups; daughter, Coral, for making straight A's; and to husband and father, Larry, for his insights and unfettered fish-eye view. "Just another day in paradise."

Salt Water Basics

SELECTING AND PURCHASING TACKLE

Purchasing the right tackle is as essential to a good day of angling as picking a locale. Tackle designed for freshwater falters quickly in a saltwater environment and has ruined more than one fishing expedition. Gear designed to withstand the elements is essential for angling the Emerald Coast waters. Rust and corrosion are the primary enemies, so avoid metal components by purchasing nylon, graphite, plastic, and fiberglass alternatives whenever possible. For those items only made of metals, such as pliers, the stainless steel versions are recommended.

As is often the case, most inland tackle shops do not carry saltwater gear. Mail-order companies are an option but testing the equipment prior to the purchase is not possible. For the beginner, I recommend waiting until you arrive to the Emerald Coast and shopping at the local bait and tackle shops. Competition is high so the prices are not inflated, and the staffs can help personalize gear according to your needs. Use the following descriptions to acquaint yourself with the functions of various saltwater tackle and help determine which items are suited for your needs.

Rod and Reel

Rods and reels are your most important purchases, but choosing the right ones can be confusing when dealing with such a saturated market. Luckily, technological advancements in recent years have enabled a single set to serve in a multitude of angling situations. The following are a few criteria to consider when making your initial purchases.

Tackle is more durable now than it used to be, allowing for the use of lighter tackle, and lighter tackle leads to a more exciting fight. For our purposes, tackle groups into two main categories: light and medium (lighter and heavier rigs are subsequent Christmas gifts). A light saltwater rod is generally 6 to 6 ¹/₂ feet long and seats a reel designed for 6- to 12-pound test line. A medium rod is slightly longer with a length between 6 ¹/₂ and 7 feet. Its reel holds line in the 12- to 20-pound class.

Factory packaged rod and reel combinations are more affordable, but purchasing the two items separately allows you to personalize. The sales people can readily inform you about correct rod and reel matches. Request rod eyes and a reel seat that are rustproof, and make sure the crank turns smoothly. However, do not be swindled into investing hundreds or thousands of dollars for your first rig. Fifty to 150 dollars is sufficient for beginners' gear. Once you're hooked, larger contributions to the bait and tackle shops become justifiable.

The three major considerations when deciding on a purchase are rod length, rod action, and reel capacity. Rod length affects casting distance and casting control. A longer rod allows a farther cast, but is quite difficult to maneuver in tight places where short casts are necessary. The 6- to 7-foot range serves both situations.

Rod action deals with the rigidity of the rod (a light rod being more flexible than a medium version). Line strength, lure weight, and anticipated fish size are all factors in determining the appropriate rod action. A light rod is more limited in the scope of fish it can land, but provides the optimal fight against a fish within its range. A medium rod has the capability to catch larger fish, but proves less exciting while landing smaller quarry. A happy medium is always best when getting started.

Reel capacity is the amount of monofilament a reel holds. This is determined by the size and style of the reel. A reel capacity of at least 250 yards is necessary when fishing along the Emerald Coast. Saltwater fish often take the bait, then run great distances before the fight begins, and a large reel capacity prevents fish from taking out all the line.

Even the highest quality gear fails when not properly maintained. Flush the rod and reel with fresh water after each use, and lubricate the reel regularly. The types of lubricants, how to apply them, and how often to use them are discussed in the directions that come with the purchases. Also, a parts list is included so you can replace worn components rather than investing in a new rig.

Those are the basic criteria for selecting a rod and reel. Now you must determine what style rig suits you best. The two popular versions of saltwater tackle are spinning and baitcasting. Each has advantages to consider, but ultimately the choice is personal preference. The following highlights the pros and cons of each.

Spinning Tackle A spinning reel is an open-faced rig mounted on the underside of a spinning style rod. This style is considered easier to operate than a baitcaster due to its ability to function with light tackle. Light lines, lures, and baits cast properly and with little possibility of backlash. Backlashing occurs when loose line gathers, twists, and tangles forming what looks like and is often referred to as a bird's nest. This is more common when using a baitcasting rig.

The spinning reel's major drawback is line twist. Line twist occurs as a fish is reeled in. This lessens the amount of pressure the monofilament can withstand and heightens the chance of a fish snapping the line. One other drawback is the inability to easily adjust the drag while simultaneously reeling. This feature is possible with a baitcaster and presents certain advantages but should not be a major consideration when purchasing your first rig.

Do not mistake spinning tackle with spincasting tackle. Spincasting implies a closed-face reel and is generally for freshwater fishing only.

Baitcasting Tackle   A baitcasting reel is an open-faced reel mounted on the top side of a baitcasting rod. Its most obvious advantage over the spinning reel is the ability to eliminate line twist during reeling, thus maintaining the strength of the monofilament during a fight. Secondly, the baitcasting rig allows you to easily increase the drag and retrieve the lure simultaneously. This keeps constant pressure against the fish and reduces its chances of spitting the hook. The baitcasting reel also provides farther casting distance than a spinning rig.

The main disadvantage of the baitcaster is backlashing. Angling with too light a lure is usually the cause—a problem not inherent with a spinning rig. Although new technologies, such as improved braking systems, have helped reduce the frequency of backlashing, the baitcaster remains notorious for this occurrence, especially for the beginner angler.

Reducing backlash becomes a matter of practice, and even the most proficient fishermen backlash from time to time using both types of rigs. In my opinion, the advantages of the baitcasting rig over the spinning rig justify the initial frustrations of learning to cast properly. Again, personal preference is the best guide when making the purchase.

The Tackle Box and What to Put inside It

The tackle box is the fisherman's briefcase, and before purchase two main points need consideration. First, the box should be rust and corrosion proof. Even the latches should be of a non-metallic construction to defend against the saltwater elements. Secondly, the tackle box should be large enough to hold all your gear. For instance, many designs do not provide ample space for an extra spool of line. Extra line, however, is an essential item for saltwater angling. Avoid purchasing too small a unit and eliminate the hassles of toting two or three cases. Buy one large enough the first time around.

What you pack into the tackle box is even more important. Being prepared for a variety of situations prevents you from running to the tackle shop while your buddy stays ocean side and reels in the big one. The following is a listing of those items necessary to enjoy a full day of fishing, as well as handle most of the unexpected dilemmas that might arise.

Monofilament Line   Monofilament line is the main link between you and the fish, and as with anything, your chain is only as strong as its weakest link. Replacing line accordingly and using it properly are essential for catching fish in the Emerald Coast waters.

A reel spooled with healthy line lands more fish. Unfortunately, monofilament line weakens by wear, weather, or twisting. A visual examination is one way to determine whether or not the line needs changing: discoloration, or graying, is a sign of weakened line. Or simply give the line a good pull. Worn-out monofilament snaps instead of stretching. Several dramatic fights weaken the monofilament, so always check it after landing a feisty fish. Also, the line on a reel that sits up for more than one year should be examined. Replace the line accordingly.

Replacing the reel with heavier test line does not mean you can catch bigger fish. Line weight should be commensurate with your rod and reel size. If you are fishing with light tackle and you expect to hook bigger fish, then use only the highest recommended line weight. Never exceed the recommended weights. Line too heavy for a reel backlashes frequently and leaves you to untangle your gear as the pompano run by.

Carry enough monofilament to re-spool your reel, as well as shorter lengths of a variety of monofilament sizes. Heavier line in the 20- to 50-pound test range is used to make leaders and are purchased by the yard at bait and tackle shops. A few yards of several weights is sufficient.

Leaders   Anglers often fish with a light line to provide better sportsmanship and a more challenging fight, but a leader is often necessary to prevent the light line from snapping. The leader enhances defense against abrasion, sharp teeth, and hard jaws and helps absorb line stress and shock. One type of leader is constructed from heavier monofilament and tagged to the reel line. Generally a leader is 12 to 24 inches long for light and medium tackle, and 5 to 10 pounds heavier than the current reel line. This type, the monofilament leader, is good for anything without serious teeth, such as redfish, speckled trout, sheepshead, and pompano.

For the serious biters, like Spanish and king mackerel, jack crevalle, barracuda, shark, and bluefish, a wire leader is highly recommended. (It is possible to catch the toothy creatures on heavy monofilament, but plan to lose a few along the way.) A wire leader should never be longer than necessary, generally about 12 to 18 inches long. The wire is attached to the monofilament with a swivel or by tying the monofilament directly to a loop-end on the leader. As with all terminal tackle, the leader should be as unnoticeable to the fish as possible. Use dull-colored wire, sleeves, and swivels.

Wire leaders can be purchased prefabricated or you can make your own. For the prefabricated ones use the sleeved versions rather than the twist versions, as they are more likely to thwart kinks. On the other hand, constructing a leader—which I discuss in pages ahead—is a very simple task that adds to the joy of fishing and reduces its expense. The cardinal rule about leaders is the lighter and less obtrusive, the more likely fish are to strike it.

Sleeves and Swivels   Sleeves are small metal collars used to tie off the leader loop. They crimp around a section of doubled-back wire and blend with the rest of the terminal tackle. They can be purchased in various sizes according to the gauge of the wire they will accompany.

Swivels are used to attach leaders, lures, and weights to lines. They also help prevent line twist and act as stoppers for slide weights. Use swivels two to three times the weight class of your line (if you're using 10-pound test line, use a swivel rated at 20 to 30 pounds). Several styles exist, but I recommend the barrel swivels. Buy a package with assorted sizes. Blacks, grays, and other dull colors are recommended to prevent spooking possible quarry. Another advantage is that bait fish attracted to shiny objects won't bite them and cut the line.

Sinkers   Sinkers come in several different styles including egg, pyramid, slip, and split-shot. They are categorized by ounce sizes and/or pound class.

Slip weights thread over the line and slide freely up and down. They usually supplement weight to a retrieved lure or bait. Egg weights are used primarily for bottom fishing and are tied off or allowed to slide freely over the line. Pyramid weights are used in similar situations as egg weights, but flat sides prevent them from being dragged across the ocean floor by currents. They are usually tied below the hook on a bottom rig.

Split-shot weights are spherical and diced halfway through for crimping to the line after the rigging is assembled. Assorted packages are your best bet, because day-to-day conditions necessitate different amounts of weight. How to use sinkers is highlighted in the upcoming section on riggings.

Floats   Floats are used to suspend a bait in the mid-waters when bottom or surface fishing is a bust. Styrofoam, cork, and plastic versions are common. Clear plastic designs are the most versatile and serve a second purpose: to create surface noise when retrieved across the water. Many plastic models can be filled with water to add weight to a rig and eliminate the need for sinkers. Another option is lighted floats, but I do not recommend these unless you have a specific purpose in mind.

Hooks and Sharpening Stone   Hooks come in an assortment of sizes and should be purchased according to the anticipated size of

the catch. For everyday gear, stock your tackle box with a pack of
2/0 hooks and an assorted package containing a range of 1/0 to 4/0
sizes.

An important differentiation in hooks is shank length. The
shank is the extension from the hook-eye to the beginning of the
hook-bend. Long shank hooks are used when baiting with shrimp.
This longer version threads delicate shrimp all the way up the hook
and helps prevent them from falling off. Short shank hooks are less
obtrusive, thus better with other baits. Fish are less likely to get
spooked by short shank hooks.

One important and commonly overlooked item for the tackle
box is a file or stone to sharpen hooks and lures. The best way to
injure or lose a fish is with a dull hook. Avoid this by sharpening
your hook ten times more often than you think is necessary.

Artificial Lures   Artificial lures come in all shapes and sizes. A
spectrum of colors, for everything from imitation crustaceans to
squid, lines the tackle shop pegboards. Certain waters require different styles, as I will illustrate in the chapters to come. A good rule
of thumb is to learn the bait fish of an area and find the lure that
best replicates them.

Of the large variety of artificial lures available, there are three
basic types. Surface lures warble along the top of the water and
draw fish that strike the shadows at the sunlit surface. Some rattle
and churn the surface to attract game. However, surface lures are
limited in use because they require a strict set of weather conditions
to be effective.

A second group is floaters, which dive when retrieved. These,
too, attract many surface feeders and, like all lures that draw fish to
the surface, provide that remarkable frenzy when the fish initially
hit and thrash out of the water.

The third group is sinking lures, or jigs, which come in an array
of designs. Jigs are the most popular for one simple reason: they
catch the most fish. For the Emerald Coast waters jigs are by far the

most diverse and efficient artificial lure. Some jigs come with skirts or ribbons that stream behind a lead head. Others are simply a lead head fitted with the grub or plastic tail of your liking. They range in size and weight according to anticipated catches and are capable of attracting nearly all species of fish. White-and-red, white-and-pink, and red-and-silver combinations work best along the Emerald Coast.

Pliers and Knife   Pliers are necessary for crimping, removing fish hooks, and for tweaking the carburetor on your 1967 Mercury outboard. A small fillet knife is handy when cutting bait fish, clipping lines, and filleting at the end of the day. An all-in-one tool, complete with pliers, knife, screwdriver, etc., is the best alternative and fits easily into the tackle box. Stainless steel versions are recommended, and generic brands are extremely affordable.

A trick of the trade is to pack a pair of fingernail clippers. They are the simplest way to clip monofilament and reduce the chance of damaging the line by incidental knife nicks.

Official Documents   Proper documents are required to fish along the Emerald Coast. Although the terms and prices change daily, some basic guidelines not likely to change are as follows. To fish in Florida, Florida residents between the ages of 16 and 65 only need a license when fishing from a boat, fishing from a spot only reachable by boat, or wade fishing in water over 5 feet deep. That means that with all shore, pier, or other stationary fishing, no license is required for residents. Nonresidents of Florida over 15 and under 65 need a license anywhere the license is not included in the fishing fee. For instance, when fishing a pier the license is often included in the walkout fee. You can purchase three-day, seven-day or annual saltwater licenses from almost any bait and tackle shop.

To fish in Alabama, residents of the state are not required to purchase a license if they are under 16 or over 64. Nonresidents are only exempt if they are younger than 16. Between the above ages, all persons are required to obtain a license before fishing anywhere in salt water. In other words, surf fishing is not free to residents or nonresidents in this state. Seven-day or annual licenses are the options.

Know the regulations. While purchasing your license, ask for the brochure with the updated specifications. It will clearly explain what fish are off limits, if any, and the weight or length ranges of those in season.

Nothing ruins a day like a costly fine. We are here to fish and to get away from our jobs so let's not bring the game warden's job to us. These guys are around to make sure the following generations will be able to land the big ones too.

Measuring device   Always carry a device for checking the weight and length of your catches to ensure they are legal to keep them. A soft tape (such as tailors use) is sufficient to measure length. Tackle shops stock several types, such as stickers for fastening to a cooler lid or the inside hull of a boat. Various kitchen scales or hand-held scales are ample for checking poundage, and bait shops carry units that measure both length and weight.

Outside the Tackle Box

A few fishing implements are too large for the tackle box. Although not essential, the following items prove beneficial, and anglers usually acquire them after their first few trips.

Lip-Gaffs, Gaffs, and Nets   Landing large fish from an elevated height, such as a boat deck or dock, is difficult and sometimes dangerous without a lip-gaff, gaff, or net. A lip-gaff is a handle with a clamp on one end that pinches the fish's lip in order to lift it from the water. Most are equipped with scales that weigh fish as they are raised. Lip-gaffs also land the fish without puncturing or maiming like a regular gaff and are the preferred tool for catching and releasing.

A gaff is a long handle with an out-turned hook jabbed into the side of a fish so it can be pulled up from the water. However, gaffs severely wound fish. Use them only for catches you plan to keep. Also, be alert when using a gaff. Fish flounce and thrash when gaffed, causing a potentially dangerous situation for an unsuspecting angler.

A net is effective for scooping small to medium catches and keeps anglers' hands away from potential sharp teeth. Whatever method you use, proper technique helps reduce the risk of complications. Read over the section concerning proper landing before your first outing.

Cooler   Always carry a cooler whether fishing from land or boat if you plan to keep your catches. Fish must either be kept alive or over ice to prevent spoiling in the heat. The cooler is also an excellent place to store live and cut bait.

Surf Fishing Spike   A section of PVC pipe 2 to 3 feet long serves as a surf fishing spike. Cut one end at a 45-degree angle for spiking into the sand. This provides the perfect stabilizer for a hands-free, unattended surf rod while fishing from the beach. Prefabricated styles are sold at local tackle shops.

Gloves and Rags   Fishing gets messy, so carry towels or rags for cleanup. Plan on donating these to the cause. You will not want them for showering purposes once they have spent a day on the beach or boat.

A second towel or pair of gloves should be set aside for releasing fish. A fish's scales and the oily film that covers them are easily damaged by bare hands. Handling the fish with a moist towel or dampened cotton gloves will reduce the risk of harming the fish. Read the section on safe release for proper handling techniques.

Maps, Charts, and Fish Finders   Fish finders are helpful for angling from a boat. Although some are quite costly, a hand-held model often proves to be an extremely accurate and affordable luxury.

Maps and depth charts of specific coastlines, bays, and water-ways are helpful for locating the flats, shelves, holes, and inlets best suited for fishing. Studying tide and current tables can also prove incredibly beneficial before venturing out. Check the local bait shops for these items.

Bait and tackle shops are stocked from tower to cellar with products guaranteed to catch the most and biggest fish. Those I include in the section "Hot Spots" scarcely scratch the surface, although they are the ones for getting started. No doubt, you will deem other items essential as you grow addicted to and eventually lend your life to angling. A bait bucket keeps bait fish and shrimp alive and lively all day. A cast net allows you to catch your own bait and refill the bait bucket. And so on. Eventually all the items you once considered luxuries will be necessities. But start with the basics and discover what else you need along the way.

HOW TO RIG YOUR OUTFIT

Saltwater fishing has, over the years, evolved through ingenuity and kept pace with technology. But with each innovation, rigging for saltwater fishing has become more and more complex. Every angler has his or her own preference as to the best knot, most successful bait, etc., and rather than overwhelming you with thirty different methods for every situation, I have compiled only the basics for rigging your outfit. The following will get you started. The rest will arrive through first-hand experience.

Knots

There are two basic types of knots. Those that attach a line to an object, such as line to lure, line to hook, or line to swivel, and those that attach one line to another. The latter knot serves to tag two lines together.

I have selected one knot for each occasion. They were chosen with two things in mind: strength and simplicity.

Palomar Knot   The Palomar knot is used to attach hooks, swivels, artificial lures, or any object to a monofilament line. A hook is used in the following steps as an example.

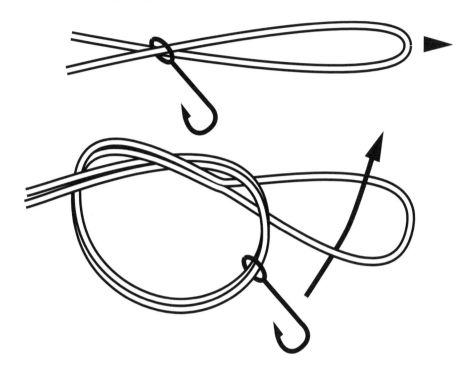

Step 1: Double-back the line to create a loop. Push the loop through the hook eye.

Step 2: Pass the loop over the line on the opposite side of the hook eye, then push it through the middle (as though tying an overhand knot).

Step 3: Slide the hook through the looped end.

Step 4: Wet the knot, then apply a steady pull to both loose ends until the line cinches just above the rod eye.

Step 5: Clip the tag end.

Blood Knot   The blood knot is used for tagging two lines together, or for tagging monofilament line to a light wire leader.

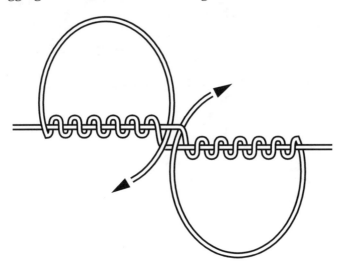

Step 1: *Overlap the two lines pointing them in opposite directions.*

Step 2: *Wrap the loose (tag) end of one line around the other five or six times, then poke the tag end through an opening between the two lines.*

Step 3: *Wrap the other tag end around the first line, then pass it through the same opening you passed the first, but in the opposite direction.*

Step 4: *Moisten the knot and apply even pressure until the line draws into a tight knot. Clip the tag ends, but leave 1/8 inch to prevent the knot from slipping during battle.*

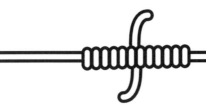

How to Make Wire Leaders

Wire leaders are essential for catching many saltwater species. They are added to the end of the monofilament to prevent toothy species from biting through the line. Prefabricated versions are sold at tackle shops, but you can minimize costs by making your own from a spool of braided wire and a packet of wire sleeves.

Step 1: *Cut a length of braided wire 18 to 36 inches, depending on the fish in the area. Take out two sleeves.*

Step 2: *Thread one loose wire end through the sleeve and double it back, leaving about a $1/4$-inch loop.*
Note: Lures, hooks, swivels, etc., must be threaded on before doubling the wire back in the second step.

Step 3: *Thread the same loose end back through the sleeve in opposite direction, and crimp the sleeve with a pair of pliers.*

Step 4: *Repeat the process on the other tag end.*

I recommend attaching a lure directly to the leader loop on one end. This eliminates a swivel and keeps the visual noise from terminal tackle to a minimum. Attach a swivel on the other end. The monofilament line is then tied to the swivel, which allows the lure to operate properly and keeps line twist to a minimum.

Note: Extra weight and beads may be added to wire leaders to enhance the casting ability of a lure. My suggestion is to keep it simple. If you need more weight purchase a heavier lure. Remember, the less obtrusive the terminal tackle the more likely the fish are to bite.

The Proper Rig

Be familiar with the proper rigs for angling in salt water whether you are casting, trolling, bottom fishing, or still fishing. Knowing how and when to use a certain rig is key for catching the quarry. However, the variety of rigs is endless, and no two fishermen are likely to agree on the best for each circumstance. In fact, most seasoned anglers have modified the basic rigs with their own bends and knots, kinks, and lengths. And as you slowly become addicted you too will find the need to experiment. Until that time arrives, the following are proven rigs for angling the occasions mentioned above. These can be purchased at many bait and tackle shops, or you can make your own. There are many good books dedicated to the art of making your own rig.

Bottom Fishing and Surf Fishing Rigs   Bottom rigs and surf rigs are similar in construction. Bottom rigs are fitted with sinkers with rounded edges, like bank or egg sinkers. The rounded edges prevent bottom rigs from hanging up on underwater structures. On the other hand, surf rigs are fitted with flat-sided sinkers, like pyramids sinkers. The flat sides keep the rig rolling or dragging across the ocean floor.

Both rigs are fished on the bottom. Surf rigs are generally positioned beyond the first wave break-in the slough between the sandbars. Bottom rigs are usually positioned in calmer waters, like bays and lakes. However, these are merely the common uses of each. Both rigs should be considered in regard to specific conditions.

Basic Rig for Surf Fishing   The basic rig for surf fishing enables the bait to move freely on its own tributary of line. This free action prevents fish from feeling the sinker as they take the bait and thus keeps them from spitting the hook before you have a chance to set it.

One technique when using this rig in the Gulf is to cast beyond the wave break and let the sinker fall to the bottom. When the sinker hits bottom crank the reel two or three turns. The sinker's weight is now on the line, which makes it easier to feel a fish bumping the bait. Swap the pyramid weight for an egg or bank weight and this rig operates as a bottom-fishing rig.

Traveling Bottom Rig for Surf Fishing   The traveling bottom rig allows the bait and line to drift with the currents. The line is threaded through the eye of a pyramid sinker and the sinker is positioned roughly 2 feet above the hook. (A swivel is attached to prevent the sinker from sliding any lower.) When in the water, the sinker anchors to the bottom, but the line moves freely through the eye and allows the bait to drift away or retrieve according to the currents. In doing so the bait covers more ground than when it is stationary. The traveling rig also keeps fish from feeling the weight of the sinker as they run with the bait, thus lessening the odds of them trying to spit the hook. This, too, can be adapted for calmer water bottom fishing by swapping the pyramid sinker for an egg sinker.

Using Live Bait

Live baits are an effective lure, but they must be more than just alive. The action of the live bait draws the game fish, so it is important that live baits be lively. Hooking them properly prolongs this liveliness and enhances your odds of drawing a strike. If a bait becomes sluggish, re-bait with a fresh one because sluggish baits do not draw game fish.

Live bait fish should range from 3 to 6 inches long. The best along the Emerald Coast include alewives, finger mullet, ronkers, cigar minnows, and bull minnows. Other live baits include shrimp, fiddler crabs, sand fleas, and blue crabs. Following are the proper ways to hook bait fish, shrimp, and cut bait.

Downward Action   When using bait fish in calm waters, place the hook through the top of the head just behind and above the eyes. Don't add weight. This hooking technique causes the fish to thrash at the surface (as it fights away from the pressure of the hook) and draws game fish to the top waters.

Down and Away Action   Hook a bait fish three-fourths of the way down its back through the fin on the top side. The fish swims downward and away from the hook. This is also good for calm waters.

Natural Action for Currents, Trolling, and Casting   Hooking bait fish through the upper lip allows them to troll, retrieve, or drift against the current in a natural manner. Make sure the hook point faces up when using this lip method. Also, pay attention as you hook the bait fish. They try to swallow the hook as you pierce the lip.

You can also hook bait fish through the eye socket. Thread the hook into one side and out the other. Do not go through the eyeball if possible—this weakens the fish and reduces its action.

Up and Away Action for Bottom Fishing   Bottom fishing with live bait works best when the bait fish is hooked three-quarters of the way back on the underside. Weight the line 2 feet up from the hook. The weight keeps the fish near the bottom, but the hook on its underside causes it to fight up and away.

Baiting with Live or Dead Shrimp   Live or dead shrimp are excellent bait in the Gulf of Mexico. Use the largest live shrimp you can find. Dead shrimp must be freshly dead. Frozen versions fail to produce the scent needed to draw the game fish. Most seafood markets sell freshly dead shrimp for angling.

A long shank hook is necessary when angling with shrimp. Live and dead shrimp are both baited in the same manner. Insert the point into the meaty spot at the base of the tail. Roll the hook forward while threading the hook shank through the torso. Exit the hook on the legged side of the body as near the neck as possible. This method hides the hook and makes it difficult for small fish to pick the shrimp off the hook.

Using Cut Bait

A short shank hook is sufficient when using cut bait. Poke the hook through the bait numerous times to prevent it from falling off or being picked off by crabs and small fish. The hook should be hidden in the cut bait.

Note: All fish species listed above as live bait fish are excellent cut baits. Also, squid is preferred in the region.

BASIC ANGLING TECHNIQUES

As an angler you are responsible for knowing everything from how to spot fish to how to properly release them. Learning these following techniques makes for a safe and fulfilling outing and benefits the sport of angling for both fish and fishermen.

Spot Fishing with Polarized Sunglasses

In spot fishing, the fisherman casts a lure toward a specimen already located in the water. This obviously differs from most other types of fishing, in which the angler casts blindly, hoping to chance upon a fish. Thus, spot fishing relies heavily on one's ability to visually locate quarry in the water, a technique best sharpened through experience. However, polarized sunglasses can be of considerable help. They are designed to reduce surface glare and allow you to see what is in the water rather than what is on it. These sunglasses are now common and can be found at corner apothecaries, gas stations, and tackle shops. Of course, not all new sunglasses are polarized, so make sure the pair you buy is advertised as *polarized.*

If you are not sure whether your current lenses are polarized, here is a simple test. Hold the lenses up to the light and twist one lens a quarter turn. Two polarized lenses held perpendicular to one another will not allow light to pass through and will appear black. If the test fails, and light continues to filter, then the suspected lenses are not polarized. In this case, purchase a pair of polarized sunglasses. No angler should be without them.

Once equipped with the proper implements you can begin to hone your spotting skills. The first step is learning to read the water, and a high vantage point is helpful for beginners. Start by standing on a sand dune, boardwalk, balcony, or any elevated structure that allows you to look down on the surf. This high vantage

provides a better angle of vision and exaggerates the various inflections in the surf.

Also, use the sun and the seasons when spot fishing. Early
morning and late afternoon, when the sun is nearer the horizon,
provide the best light for spotting fish. Turn your back to the sun
and use the light's low trajectory to illuminate the underwater. The
spring and autumn are the best seasons for spot fishing. Schooling
fish run west to east in the fall and east to west in the spring.
Therefore, spotting in the spring is best with a setting sun because
you are watching for oncoming fish with the light at your back. In
the fall a morning sun is prime.

Using the high vantage (and sun and seasons when applicable),
examine the area of surf along and inside the first sandbar. Notice
the overall look of the water. Is it yellowish? More greenish? Brown?
Notice the areas that appear slightly darker than the mean. These
are the sloughs, washes, and other low spots along the bottom.
Now concentrate on a smaller section of the surf (about 50 feet in
diameter). Do you see any darker patterns? Shadows? Gray areas?
These differences will seem very subtle at first. Check thoroughly,
and if you see nothing peculiar, move to another section. If you do
notice something, keep an eye on the inflection. Is it moving? Is it
changing size or shape? Things embedded in the ocean floor generally only waver. Pass these by. Inflections that drift, surge, or move
parallel to the coastline could be fish. Take a closer look.

A drifting action may simply reveal seaweed or other debris, but
do not jump to that conclusion yet. Make a mental note of the
shadow and check it from time to time for movement. Sometimes
fish drift in the currents and wait for bait fish to swim to them, and
the shadows of seaweed turn out to be cobia. A shadow that surges
or moves parallel to the coastline is usually a fish. Fish these by
casting over the shadow and retrieving the lure so that it crosses in
front of the fish.

Fish are spotted in the waves also. They lurk in the bellies of
waves waiting to ambush bait. Watch the belly of a wave as it rolls
up just before its crests. Sunlight illuminates the wave as it rises and

large shadows of fish appear, usually in singles, pairs, or pods.

Spotting a school of fish is an easier task than spotting individual specimens. Schools appear as large, dark shadows moving parallel to the coastline and are particularly prevalent in the spring and autumn. Some shadows appear to swell and condense. Others show white water splashing at the surface. Sometimes these schools turn out to be mullet, a herbivorous species. Common baits will not lure them. But do not get frustrated. Mullet are a favorite feast of many game fish. Find them and the game fish are not far behind.

After you feel comfortable with these techniques from the high vantage, practice them at beach level, then from the surf. Before long you will be casting at pods from waist-deep water and spotting schools miles down the coastline.

Casting

Casting accurately is essential for catching fish consistently. This accuracy is best achieved through repetition. For the beginner, practicing your cast saves the frustration of hanging up in a limb or throwing a lure shy of a 75-pound cobia. Landlocked persons can use the backyard as a practice area before venturing out. Tie a $1/2$-ounce sinker to the end of your line, pick a target on the far side of the lawn, and throw until you consistently come within a 3-foot radius of the target. Use only a sinker when doing this exercise to ensure a snag-free retrieve. If water is easily accessible, pick a particular section of water and practice casting using a top-water artificial lure. That way you can also watch and learn how the lure behaves when retrieved.

With enough practice you will land the lure within a few feet of an intended target every time. Also, you will begin to deviate somewhat from the traditional overhand cast and slip into a more personalized style. Usually your angle of trajectory is somewhere between the overhead and the side-arm cast. Continue working this cast, as well as experimenting with a variety of angles, until the motions become fluent. Now, when dealing with a less conventional angling spot, like one with low-lying limbs, placing a bait accordingly is second nature.

Retrieving

Retrieving a lure involves more than just cranking the reel. To begin, the typical cast requires taking out the slack in the line before beginning the retrieve (especially when casting into the wind). Once the bait enters the water, raise the rod tip to its highest point, then reel in as you return the rod tip to waist level. Taking out the slack in this manner tightly winds the line around the spool, thus minimizing the possibility of backlash occurring on subsequent casts.

After this initial slack is removed, you can either use a straight retrieve (reeling in without adding action to the lure) or add a series of stalls and jigs to enhance the lure's action. To stall, or stop reeling, the retrieve will cause a lure to pause, and, in most cases, sink. Jigging, or jerking, the rod tip while retrieving pulls the lure in short, quick spurts. The two techniques are used separately or in a variety of combinations. Exactly how to manipulate each retrieve depends on particular water conditions, types of fish sought, and the style of lure being drawn. Just keep in mind that the idea is to mimic the movement of a bait fish. The ability to do so is often the difference between missing and hooking a fish. The following are examples on how to retrieve spoons, plugs, and jigs.

Spoons   Spoons, popular saltwater lures, range widely in shape, size, and color but are typically a metal blade, roughly the shape of a kitchen spoon's head, with a single hook on the underside. Gold and silver are the common colors.

A moderate to slow retrieve is most effective when using spoons along the Emerald Coast. This keeps them near the surface to draw species that climb fast and strike near the top. Spoons are designed to wobble and flash during a straight, steady reel. The action is felt as vibrations traveling up the line and down the pole. These are subtle, but noticeable. Failure to feel this action means the retrieve is the wrong tempo. Speed up or slow down accordingly.

Jigging causes spoons to spurt forward and rise. Stalling and lowering the rod tip makes spoons flutter and sink. Add this action to spoons only when water visibility is poor. On clear days spoons produce ample action with a straight reel, and additional action only spooks game fish and prevents them from approaching.

Plugs Plugs are an equally popular artificial lure for salt water. Most simulate a wounded bait fish or a bait fish struggling in the water. Styles vary from torpedoes to poppers to swimmers, most of which draw fish by creating surface commotion, like splashing or rippling.

Popping plugs work best when retrieved quickly. Supplement the reeling by jigging the rod tip, then holding the plug steady on the surface. Repeat the process throughout the retrieve. Work a torpedo plug in a similar manner but make the jigging actions fuller so the plug skips across the water before pausing. Swimmers are another effective style of plug. Draw them rapidly through the water, allowing the plastic lip to splash along the surface and attract nearby game. Or use a moderate to slow retrieve so that they snake along the surface and create an enticing wake for fish striking from below.

Also, a number of plugs are designed to swim at various depths. These underwater plugs usually dive when retrieved and lowering or raising the rod tip changes their depths accordingly. Overall, plugs are an effective lure along the Emerald Coast, although some versions fail to lend the excitement of the surface strike.

Jigs The best artificial lures for Emerald Coast fishing are jigs. They come in several different styles, but those with lead heads and frayed nylon tails are preferred. Red, white, pink, yellow, and silver are the proven colors for attracting a variety of species.

Jigs are versatile. They can reach deep water regardless of currents or stay near the surface when retrieved swiftly. Slow retrieves work for some bottom feeders, like flounder, but fast retrieves work better for most saltwater game fish. Jigging, or rapidly jerking the rod, during either type of retrieve lures almost anything in the vicinity. Stock your tackle box with jigs. They are the ultimate bait for saltwater fishing.

Always remember, lures are designed to imitate bait fish. Make your lure look as lively and realistic as the bait fish in the area and fish will strike consistently.

The Strike

Perhaps the most thrilling moment for a fisherman is the hard, fast strike before the line peels from the reel. The slack evades, the rod bows, your knuckles whiten. Instinct tells you to yank back and fight opposite the fish's pull. But this is not always the case. Many saltwater fish have soft mouths. Jerking the rod too hard rips their flesh and releases the hook. Other hard-mouthed species sound, or dive, to the deep water with such force that a hard set straightens the hook under the strain. Other fish simply take the hook with such force that setting the hook only increases the chance of fouling your rig. Hooking fish is a matter of knowing what reaction to the strike provides the best results.

How to react to a strike depends on what type of fish is biting. Chapter 4, "Fish Species, Habitats, and Angling Techniques," provides information on reeling in particular species, including how to set the hook and how to fight them. Of course, incidental catches occur, and certain basic techniques can be applied to all species. Setting the hook properly is the initial concern.

Setting the Hook

Setting the hook is a tricky matter. Some fish have hard bony mouths, like sheepshead. These types of species usually bump lightly at first while testing the bait. Let them test the bait, and use a hard jerk or series of jerks to set the hook—only after you feel a strong, steady pull. A hard jerk is essential to penetrate their tough mouths.

Other species grab the bait and run. Redfish behave in this manner. They swim away from the competition, removing slack in the line. Let them run with it. This elapse of time allows the quarry to swallow the bait. Set the hook when the slack dissolves and the line becomes taut, using a hard, steady pull. This action causes the fish to surge, driving the hook even deeper.

No hook set is necessary for species like mackerel and bluefish. They dart and strike with such a vengeance that maintaining constant tension throughout the fight is sufficient to keep them on the line.

Fighting

Once the hook is set the true fight begins. To fight a fish and win you need to understand a few key concepts: drag (and how to use it), counteracting, and pumping.

Drag is the amount of resistance the line has against the fish. The correct drag should be set before you cast. A general ratio is to set the drag roughly three-quarters of the line weight. For example, 9 pounds of drag is sufficient for 12-pound test line. You can estimate the drag by freehand pulling the line. Try to imagine the amount of force needed to move a 9-pound weight. If this seems difficult, tie the line to a scale and dial the drag until the line releases at 9 pounds of pressure.

Do not be afraid to adjust the drag as necessary when a fish is hooked. For instance, the tackle can break if the rod is doubled over and no line is zinging off the reel. Loosen the drag. On the other hand, tighten the drag if the fish is peeling line off the spool with ease. The rod and line do not provide the proper amount of resistance when the drag is too loose. Optimally the drag should be adjusted to provide the maximum resistance against the fish without snapping the gear. Experience develops your feel for this happy medium. And remember, fish do win the fight from time to time. Do not get frustrated if one breaks the line.

While you are setting the drag you must keep tension against the fish. Keeping the rod tip up provides the most resistance and keeps the fish from getting slack in the line. Slack in the line is an easy out for the fish, so make sure to maintain tension throughout the fight.

Counteracting is necessary for properly landing a fish, but its premise is intuitive to most people. To counteract is to adjust the line's tension in order to fight opposite the fish. For example, if the fish breaks right, lower your rod tip to about a 45-degree angle and pull to the left. This increases tension against the fish by assisting the drag with the leverage of the pole. Think about it as always fighting away from the fish.

Eventually the fish begins to tire. (The time period varies greatly according to the species and its size.) Now you must retrieve the line the fish has taken. Sometimes just reeling retrieves line, but pumping is usually necessary for the larger specimens. To pump, hold the rod tip high, then lower it parallel to the water while simultaneously reeling in the line slack. Return the rod tip steadily to the upright position and feel the resistance as the fish draws closer. Lower the rod tip again and reel the slack. Pumping is a slow but proven method. Be patient. A fish may sound two or three times before tiring, and many large ones take hours to land. Just repeat the process until the fish comes into sight, at which point you should begin preparing to land it.

Landing

Knowing when and how to land a fish properly is imperative to completing the catch. A fish is ready to land only when completely played out, or no longer green. The largest trout I almost caught was 2 feet away when it winked at me, snapped the line, and dove away. I tried to land a fish that was still green. This is a common mistake. Fish that are still fighting should be left in the water. Keep the line long enough to prevent them from tangling with the boat, and maintain steady tension by counteracting its movements until it tires out. But remember, the longer the quarry is on the line the greater its chance of escape. Trial and error helps you discover the balance.

Different fishing locales require different landing techniques. The easiest method when surf fishing is to drag the catch ashore. If you are hooked into a big one, prevent getting it caught in the undertow. These back currents, combined with the weight of the fish, are enough to snap the line. Work the line so that the fish rides to shore on an incoming wave.

In-water landings are another option for those fishing in the surf. Some people recommend short gaffs here, but gaffs are not a practical item to carry when wrestling the currents. You are better off bare-handing the catch. Make sure the fish is completely played out, then reach into the water and firmly clamp your hand either around the area just behind the head (making sure not to get gigged by a fin) or between the tail and dorsal fin. Make sure to avoid the mouth. Use your other hand to free the hook. As a note, I do not advocate in-water landings for novices. Saltwater fish thrash and bite. Take the time to beach the fish and avoid possible injuries.

Landing fish while angling from elevated heights, like boat decks and jetties, can be more difficult. Smaller catches can simply be reeled up, but larger species, capable of snapping the pole or line, must be netted or gaffed. Do not spook a fish while netting. Lower the net in the water away from the fish, move it slowly underwater toward the fish, then scoop up and around. Be as calm as possible throughout the process or the fish may flounce and break the line.

Lip gaffs are better than standard gaffs for both angler and fish, especially when releasing the catch. When using a lip gaff, hold the line taut and keep upward tension on the fish. This draws its mouth toward the surface. Extend the gaff down and clamp around the lip, keeping a firm grip on the gaff handle. Draw the fish upward and disengage the hook. A typical gaff is effective too, but only when keeping the catch. Do not use this device if you are inexperienced. Find a seasoned angler to assist you if gaffing is your only option.

Keeping or Releasing

Keeping or releasing a fish should be a conscientious decision. We must all think ecologically, as the number of people angling the Emerald Coast waters continues to increase. The quality of a fish diminishes rapidly once pulled from the water. Keep fish only if you plan to eat them in the next day or two and they are of legal limit. Release the rest. The more we leave in the ocean, the better our odds of catching one.

Make the decision to keep or release a fish prior to landing it (with the exception of the occasional wall-hanger). Fish that endure long fights are likely to be wounded. Land quarry to be released as quickly as possible and handle with great care.

The ideal release occurs without ever removing the fish from the water. Stabilize the fish in the water with a lip gaff. (A firm grip serves to stabilize smaller species.) Clamp the pliers on the hook shank and work the hook out by pushing down and away from the angle of entry. The down motion releases the barb, and the away motion slides out the point.

Often the fish must be pulled from the water in order to free the hook. In this case, lay the fish on a towel and secure it with a wetted cotton glove or moist towel. The glove or towel reduces the removal of scales and skin-surface oils imperative to the survival of the fish. Use a firm grip to prevent flouncing and avoid injury to you or the fish. Work the hook out as suggested above, and keep out-of-water time minimal. Be gentle with a hook set deep in the fish's mouth. Cut the line if the hook will not release and is causing internal damage. Cut the line as closely to the fish as possible and return the fish to the water. Over time the hook will work itself out.

To release, place the fish gently into the water. Lively specimens dart away quickly. Catches that show signs of exhaustion need help reintroducing oxygen into their gills. One way to reintroduce oxygen is to torpedo the fish into the water using a downward motion, much like spiking a football. Although it sounds unorthodox, torpedoing the fish into the water rushes water through the gills and replenishes depleted oxygen. Resilient fish, like mackerel and pompano, respond to this method. Extremely exhausted fish need more attention.

For a fish showing little sign of life, help it through the reviving process. Hold the catch between the tail and dorsal fin, and push and pull the fish through the water until it begins to wriggle. This method jump starts the fish by slowly working oxygen back into the system. The fish will swim out of your grip when sufficiently revived.

Dealing with keepers is simple. Keep them in live wells or pack them on ice. Without ice, they spoil quickly in the heated clime of the Emerald Coast. Whatever your method, make sure you know the size and weight limits prior to your trip.

SPECIAL TECHNIQUES

The following special techniques extend beyond those necessary for a great day of angling. Most require a specific set of conditions. Incorporate them when necessary as you hone your angling skills.

Cutting a Butterfly Bait

Cutting a dead bait fish into a 'butterfly' is a technique that enhances its action, thus raising the probability of drawing strikes from game fish. The technique works best on bait fish with large flanks, like pinfish and alewives. Finger mullet or minnows are not recommended. The procedure is simple.

Step 1: Insert the blade edge of a fillet knife at the bait fish flank near the tail fin.
Step 2: Slice down to the spine.

Step 3: *Pivot the blade and cut toward the head slicing the flank away from the bones. Stop the cut just before reaching the pectoral fin. Leave the flank attached.*
Step 4: *Repeat the process on the other side.*
Step 5: *With the flanks cut, remove the backbone by cutting the spine near the pectoral fin.*
Step 6: *Remove the skeletal frame.*

The bait is ready to be refastened onto the hook. When in the currents, the loose flanks will waver, adding the needed visual action. Also, this wavering releases oils and blood into the immediate waters. Both actions increase the odds of luring game fish.

Chumming

Chumming is the method of placing cut baits in the water to leave a trail, or slick, for luring game fish to an area. The practice is valuable for luring quarry when properly orchestrated. Done wrong, it can foul a perfectly splendid day of angling. The art to proper chumming is best learned through experience, but a few pointers on why to chum, when to chum, and what to chum with can help you get a head start.

The obvious reason for chumming is to draw quarry to the area you are fishing. A second, more valuable reason is to keep fish in the area once they have arrived. Selecting and preparing the proper chum produces these results.

Many different types of chum are effective. Fish remains (heads and innards) work well and are usually free to early birds waiting at the docks when the charters return from their morning runs. This type of chum is also sold in frozen blocks at most seafood markets. The downfall is they spoil rapidly and must be used that day. A more versatile option is to chum with dry dog food or cat food. An ample amount of either can be kept indefinitely on the boat or in the tackle box without spoiling. Try mixing canned sardines with the pet food. Neither spoil, and the canned sardines enhance the scent, thus making the chum more effective.

Once the ingredients are selected, prepare the chum. Mix the sardines and dog food into a softball-sized ball. (No preparation is needed for fish remains.) Place the chum in a mesh bag with approximately 1/8-inch holes. Cinch the bag shut, tie it to the boat and submerge it in the water. If you are fishing without a boat, set the chum bag in the current but keep it anchored to a stationary object so it does not drift away.

Chumming works best when currents percolate through the bag and release a moderate amount of scent and particles. The method will not work in stagnant water or in swift currents. The former fails to disperse. The latter dilutes the scent and proves ineffective. A medium current or a slow trolling speed produces the desired chum trail. The chum trail should be just strong enough to lead game fish to your bait. With too strong a trail, fish feed on the chum rather than following it to your bait. On the other hand, with too weak a trail, fish fail to pick up the scent. Experiment to find the happy medium.

As a courtesy do not chum in populated waters. Isolated areas and areas that do not attract swimmers are preferred. Sharks and other game fish do not mingle well with spring breakers.

Gigging

At certain times of year the bays and Gulf are stocked with flounder. Autumn along the Emerald Coast is the best. Flounder gather near the shore and a north wind keeps the surf and inland waters flat for easy wading. The conditions are prime for nighttime gigging.

Gigging is a common technique for catching flat fish usually done at night when fish are less active. A few items not commonly found in the tackle box are required. The gigging device, or gig, is a pole with pitchfork-like prongs on one end used for stabbing fish. The prongs are barbed to help prevent fish from sliding off once stabbed. Another essential for gigging at night is a lantern. Electric, kerosene, floating, and underwater versions are available. Also, shoes are recommended to thwart the bites of creatures lurking in the dark waters. (Some people gig from a skiff while poling through the flats. Shoes are not essential in this situation.)

Most commonly gigging takes place at night in lakes, surf, and other wading waters, and Gulf flounder are the prime target along the Emerald Coast. Wade into the water and shine the lantern down to illuminate the ocean floor. Search the floor for fish, particularly flounder, which remain motionless in the calm, night waters. Once a game fish is located, stab the prongs of the gig through the fish, using a downward motion. The fish is now pinned between the gig and the ocean floor. Reach into the water and slide your hand under the fish to ensure the catch does not slide off. Pull the fish from the water, and place it in a bucket, bag, or cooler. Do not gig fish unless you plan to keep them, as gigging causes fatal wounds.

Gigging is an excellent supplement to rod and reel fishing. Autumn waters often produce enough fish to fill a cooler in an hour. But remember to watch for nighttime predators, and keep only what you will eat.

Casting a Net

Learning to cast a net properly is valuable for two reasons. First, you can catch bait fish. Secondly, you can catch herbivorous species, such as mullet, that will not bite typical lures or baits.

Cast nets come in a variety of sizes. The most common and affordable are gauged for catching bait fish. Other, more durable makes offer the strength necessary for netting mullet and other, larger game. However, larger fish are occasionally caught in bait fish nets, but damage usually occurs to the netting. If you plan to use your net primarily for mullet or larger species, purchase one sufficient for handling the larger game.

Spotting and throwing and *blind throwing* are two methods when casting a net. When spotting and throwing, you first locate the bait fish in the water, then throw the net over them. In blind throwing you cast the net at no particular target with hopes of getting lucky. Both techniques are successful and usually conducted while wading or while spotting from a higher structure, such as a bridge.

There are several techniques for throwing the net properly. The following technique provides excellent results by spreading the net wide and getting full use of its circumference. The technique can be difficult to learn, but practice makes perfect. After a while casting a net will become second nature.

(This is written for right-handers. Left-handers should adjust accordingly.)

Step 1: *Tie the tag end of the rope to your left wrist and coil it in the fashion shown. Hold the net at the top so the weighted end dangles near the ground.*

Step 2: *Grab the net near the midpoint with your right hand, then transfer it to your left hand, making sure to separate the net from the coiled rope by threading it between your middle and index fingers.*

Step 3: *Reach down and grab the weighted edge of the net, pulling it up and holding it between your teeth. Grab the weighted end again about an arm's length down from the section between your teeth. Note: Notice the idea is to have the net partially spread before the release.*

Step 4: *Now you are ready to throw. Point your right hip at the intended target. Pivot your hips left and back and bring your hands back to spring-load the net.*

Step 5: *Recoil forward, releasing the rope and net from your left hand in the direction of the intended target. Keep holding with your teeth and right hand. The net will begin to fan out as it opens in a circular fashion. Release the net after the perimeter of the net is fully expanded but before it snags.*

Step 6: The net will splash down and the weights will sink to the bottom. (The weights work in a manner to pre- vent anything from escaping out the open side of the net.) Now retrieve the net by pulling the rope tied to your wrist.

Step 7: Lift the net out of the water and examine your catch. Keep needed bait fish in a live well or bait bucket. Release all unwanted catches.

Filleting

Filleting is a messy job. A large, hard cutting surface located outdoors is necessary. You will need a sharp fillet knife, plus a bucket or garbage bag for disposing waste. Also, a hose keeps the filleting surface clean while you work.

Electric knives make the process easier. The type commonly used in the kitchen works as well as those sold in angling catalogs. Different fish require different filleting techniques. Some need no preparation at all. The following method is common and can be applied to most saltwater species.

Step 1: Lay the fish on the cutting surface and insert the blade edge at the flank on the anterior side of the pectoral fin. Cut down to the bone.

Step 2: Raise the blade slightly off the bone and pivot it 90 degrees so that the edge is facing the fish's tail. Slice down the lateral line separating the flank as closely to the bones as possible without cutting into them. Stop about 1 inch from the caudal fin as the flank begins to taper and the blade begins to rise toward the surface. Do not exit the blade forward. Pull it out, leaving the skin attached near the tail so that the flank dangles.

Step 3: Flop the flank over and away from the fish's head. Insert the blade edge about 1 inch up the meat near the tail.

> *Step 4*: *Slice under the meat and above the skin, working the blade as close to the skin as possible without cutting through it. Run the blade until it exits at the end.*
> *Step 5*: *Flip the fish and repeat the process.*

Wash the flanks thoroughly in the kitchen sink after filleting. Run water over the meat and massage out all the blood, dark spots, and other impurities.

Fish may be bagged and frozen, but I recommend keeping only what you will eat in the immediate future. Fish quality depreciates rapidly when frozen.

Note: I suggest cooking all quarry. Some may be best when landed, filleted, and eaten raw, but if you are not trained in such matters, cook them thoroughly. Some fish may be hosts to harmful parasites that do not die off until cooked at a certain temperature.

How to Pick a Prime Location

The Gulf of Mexico is teeming with game fish year-round, and picking a prime location is the key to locating them day after day. Understanding a few basic principles concerning the tides and currents, winds and water, and geography will enable you to consistently find the fish hidden within the Emerald Coast waters.

TIDES AND CURRENTS

Tides and currents are often overlooked by the weekend fisherman, yet a knowledge of the tides is as vital to a great day of angling as the correct lure. However, the typical rules governing tides fail once you enter the northern Gulf of Mexico. Typically, tides run on a six-hour rotation, thus four tide changes occur in a single day. However, the Gulf is prone to a sporadic cycle. Some days, two tide changes occur. Other days there are one to three. The best resolution is to stop by the local tackle shop and pick up a table listing the times of the highest and lowest waters. They are usually free.

A tide is either ebbing, flooding, or slack. An ebbing tide is outgoing, a flooding tide is incoming, and the time period (about one hour) at which the currents are neither ebbing nor flowing is a slack tide. Understanding these time periods allows you to avoid the lulls and fish the prime times.

The slack tides are regarded as the worst time of day for fishing. The waters are neither pulling nor pushing. The bait fish swim freely and unfettered by opposing currents and have little difficulty escaping the ambushes of game fish. Waiting an hour, until the tide begins to move again, eliminates the frustration of catching only a sunburn as you wade the idle waters.

The onsets of outgoing and incoming tides are the best times to fish, especially in the surf. The bait fish fall to the mercy of the shifting currents as they are pushed and pulled against their will. They also tend to school in larger groups at these times, and game fish move in to take advantage.

The last hour of an outgoing tide is another excellent time for angling. Weary game fish have had plenty of time to examine their prey, and as the tide nears the end of its cycle, they feel a sense of urgency to feed. They move in from the holes and sloughs, often chasing lures into the sandy shallows with confidence.

There are always exceptions. For instance, some locations are best during higher waters, because at low tide the area is too shallow to draw the game fish. Other spots are best during the low tide, because the shallows create more white water as the waves move over the bars and reefs. Spring and neap tides also affect the degree of rise or drop in the water, but these are things you will learn along the way. As a general rule, the hour before and the hour after the slack tides, whether ebbing or flowing, prove to be the best times for hooking game.

WINDS AND WATER

Wind and water conditions affect angling as much as currents and tides. Clear, dirty, cloudy, and perfect water are the four typical water conditions, and each is usually the result of a particular type of wind or storm.

Clear water defines a condition when the surf has been light and winds have been offshore or nonexistent for several days. The water is flat and transparent. With the waves flattened and the silt settled, the fish are wise to a leader and lure retrieved through the water. This may also be referred to as calm water or champagne water, although, due to the quality of fishing produced at this time, I find it better understood as near beer.

Dirty water refers to surf cluttered with seaweed, kelp, silt, and other aquatic debris. Drawing a lure through these water conditions usually results in hooking vegetation, thus foiling any chance of luring a fish. Cut and live baits usually go unseen. These conditions arise from offshore storms and extreme inshore winds. The best option is to wait them out and hope the waters clear.

Occasionally people use the term dirty water to describe water with a high concentration of suspended sand particles. Better referred to as cloudy water, these conditions can be favorable for certain species attracted to noisy baits, such as top-water plugs. If the conditions have been cloudy for a lengthy period, the fish are likely to become desperate and daring and begin taking baits more readily. This is especially true if the water is beginning to clear and the game fish have not been able to locate a meal through the murky water for a lengthy period. Fishing in cloudy water conditions is usually good.

Perfect water conditions are usually referred to as white water. White water signifies enough surface action in the water to create breaks over the sand bars and shoals and to obscure the water surface. This type of water draws the bait fish, hence the larger fish move in for feeding. The best fishing is usually during white water conditions.

GEOGRAPHY

Knowing the geography of the ocean floor is an essential tool in locating fish in the Emerald Coast waters. Fish tend to move with the flow of water, which is directly influenced by the terrain of the ocean floor. Sand bars, breaks, sloughs, and points are the basic underwater terrain. Thus, by locating these, you can locate the game fish.

There are two major sand bars that run along the Emerald Coast. The first runs roughly 60 feet from shore and the second bar another 100 feet beyond the first. You can locate these by watching where the waves break or by noting the lighter stripes running parallel to the coastline. The far side of the second bar is often referred to as the wall, which is where the shelf drops off into deeper waters. Fish hover along this edge. The deeper water between the two sand bars is known as the slough.

Sloughs are deep enough to draw game fish from beyond the second sand bar. Some cruise the slough, especially during the migratory seasons, and feed on the run. Other species hole up in the deep waters, waiting for bait fish to exit the shallows. In both cases, the slough is an excellent place to fish, especially when the bait is placed near a break.

Breaks are cuts in the sand bars. To locate these take note of the wave break, then see if one particular area along the coastline is not causing a wave break. The water appears flat over breaks in the sand bar as there is no underwater formation to make the wave rise and roll. These breaks provide channels for game fish to enter and exit the slough. Fish are more likely to spot a bait positioned in the slough near a break than anywhere else in the slough.

Points are another important geographic feature. A point is an underwater peninsula that extends from shore into the water. The formation is higher in elevation than the surrounding terrain, caus-ing the water to sweep around it. Where this sweeping action occurs is called a wash. Game fish, following the currents, cruise through the wash and around the point. Fish from the point and position a bait in the deepest areas of the wash. The shallow waters over these points provide an excellent area to wade out and cast into the sloughs and breaks.

The main idea, no matter where you fish, is to learn to locate irregularities in the terrain. Find these irregularities by studying the waters at low tide, and return at high tide to see how the various ocean floor inflections affect the flow of currents. After a short time the process will become second nature, as will identifying water conditions, winds, currents, and tides. Instinct will then lead you to the fish, and hooking them will follow.

CHAPTER 3

40 Hot Spots

Each Hot Spot is followed by a list of fish species, dates, and baits. These lists show the fish most likely to be hooked in the given area, the best time of year to catch them, and the preferred baits to lure them. But other species will be hooked, different times of year will prove successful, and alternate baits will be more prosperous on certain days. Use the lists as a reference for the common conditions of the areas, but not as something infallible—the possibilities are endless when fishing any spot in the Emerald Coast waters.

HOT SPOTS WEST OF US 331

Gulf Shores to Pensacola (See map on page 44)

1) Little Lagoon Pass
Directions: *From US 331 turn west onto US 98. Pass through Gulf Breeze into Pensacola and onto Gregory Street. Follow the signs to US 98 west. Take US 98 to County Road 292 and turn south. Cross onto Perdido Key. Take County Road 182 through Gulf Shores to West Pass, or Little Lagoon Pass.*

West Pass remains Little Lagoon's only outlet to the Gulf of Mexico. All quarry entering or exiting must travel through this small tributary. Parking and fishing are permitted on both sides of the small bridge that fords the waterway, but take note of the signs stating where fishing is and is not allowed.

Moving north, grass beds grow along the bend as the land begins to give way the lagoon. Trout and red drums hunt in the shallows here, and larger bullreds cruise the channel just offshore foraging mollusks and oysters on the bottom. During season, mackerel, blue runners, and other migratory species move from the Gulf through the pass scouring the waters for food. Alewives produce consistent strikes from all of the above species. Lip-hook them to keep them lively and to keep re-baiting minimal.

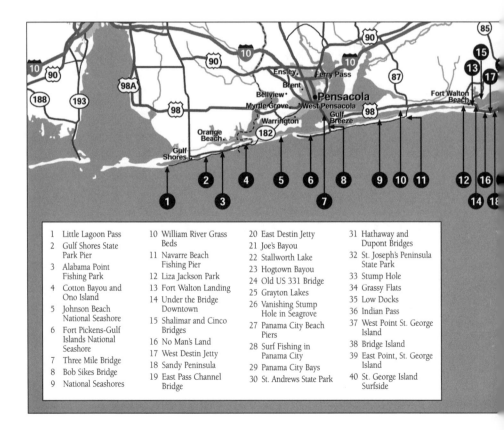

1 Little Lagoon Pass	10 William River Grass Beds	20 East Destin Jetty	31 Hathaway and Dupont Bridges
2 Gulf Shores State Park Pier	11 Navarre Beach Fishing Pier	21 Joe's Bayou	32 St. Joseph's Peninsula State Park
3 Alabama Point Fishing Park	12 Liza Jackson Park	22 Stallworth Lake	33 Stump Hole
4 Cotton Bayou and Ono Island	13 Fort Walton Landing	23 Hogtown Bayou	34 Grassy Flats
5 Johnson Beach National Seashore	14 Under the Bridge Downtown	24 Old US 331 Bridge	35 Low Docks
6 Fort Pickens-Gulf Islands National Seashore	15 Shalimar and Cinco Bridges	25 Grayton Lakes	36 Indian Pass
7 Three Mile Bridge	16 No Man's Land	26 Vanishing Stump Hole in Seagrove	37 West Point St. George Island
8 Bob Sikes Bridge	17 West Destin Jetty	27 Panama City Beach Piers	38 Bridge Island
9 National Seashores	18 Sandy Peninsula	28 Surf Fishing in Panama City	39 East Point, St. George Island
	19 East Pass Channel Bridge	29 Panama City Bays	40 St. George Island Surfside
		30 St. Andrews State Park	

Live shrimp and sand fleas are prime targets for all quarry in the Emerald Coast waters. Attach a float to your line roughly 2 to 3 feet above a live shrimp and cast into the middle of the pass. This lures fish entering and exiting the lagoon. If the fishing is slow, adjust the float and work the bait at various depths. Some fish strike from below, necessitating a bait nearer the surface. Others hit from the top, such that a lower bait works better. Experiment until you locate the game, and stick with it until the fishing slows.

> *Blue Runners: Spring, Fall—spoons, jigs*
> *Spanish Mackerel: April through June, September through*
>   *November—spoons*
> *Pompano: March through May, September to November—jigs*
> *Bluefish: March to November—live bait, jigs*

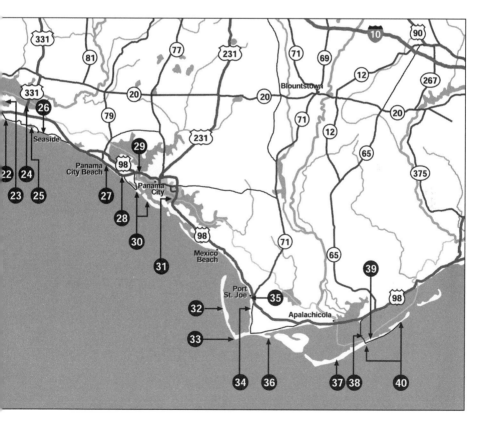

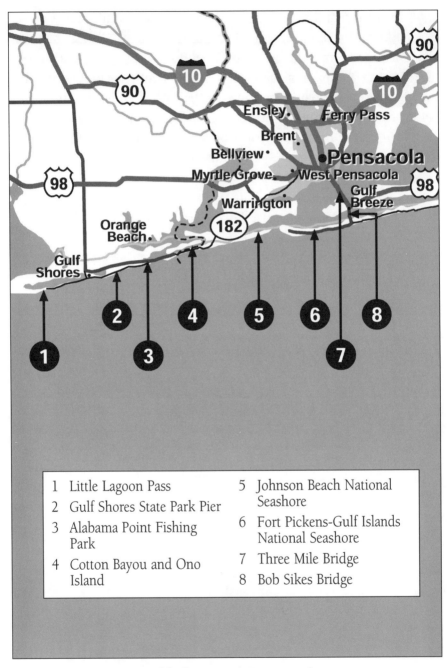

1 Little Lagoon Pass
2 Gulf Shores State Park Pier
3 Alabama Point Fishing Park
4 Cotton Bayou and Ono Island

5 Johnson Beach National Seashore
6 Fort Pickens-Gulf Islands National Seashore
7 Three Mile Bridge
8 Bob Sikes Bridge

Gulf Shores to Pensacola

2) Gulf Shores State Park Pier

Directions: *From US 331 turn west onto US 98. Pass through Gulf Breeze into Pensacola and onto Gregory Street. Follow the signs to US 98 west. Take US 98 to County Road 292. Turn south onto County Road 292 and cross over to Perdido Key. Take County Road 182 to the Gulf Shores State Park Pier on your left.*

The Gulf Shores State Park Pier is the only fishing structure extending into Alabama's share of the Gulf of Mexico. A fee is charged, but a blanket license is included. No other license is necessary. Competition is high, and anglers hoping for a shot at the bigger game fish should show at dawn and claim a spot near the end of the pier. King and Spanish mackerel, cobia, bluefish, and barracuda strike in these deeper waters. Mullet or pinfish about 6 to 8 inches long lure these larger game fish. Artificial lures draw hits, too. Oversized jigs and silver spoons are the most effective styles, and tipping these with cut bait increases your odds by adding scent to the visual allure.

Anglers arriving later can expect plenty of space over the slough that runs between the first and second sand bars. Schooling species cruise this gap during spring and autumn, and from the high vantage you can watch them approach. Pompano, bluefish, and jacks strike hard on sand fleas and shrimp and tear into short, sporadic runs. Suspend these baits in the mid-waters to entice these species that take their meals on the go. Bump the rod tip as game fish enter the vicinity to add action to a lethargic bait (live shrimp lose their action quickly). Jigs are the optimal artificial lure, although the increased height of the pier alters the action and draws it out of the water after only a short retrieve.

Sailcats are always an option from piers. Fish over the first sand bar, or just beyond it, using cut bait. Use a flat-sided sinker, like a pyramid, to hold the bait to the floor and prevent the currents from sweeping it to shore. Although not considered a game fish, sailcats fight as hard as most game.

Check out Hot Spot 34 for additional information on angling piers.

> **Spanish Mackerel:** *April through June, September through November—spoons*
> **King Mackerel:** *June to September—live bait fish*
> **Spadefish:** *June to August—live shrimp, sand fleas*
> **Flounder:** *October to March—live shrimp, grubs*
> **Pompano:** *March through May, September to November—jigs*
> **Bluefish:** *March to November—live bait, jigs*

3) Alabama Point Fishing Park

Directions: *From US 331 turn west onto US 98. Pass through Gulf Breeze into Pensacola and onto Gregory Street. Follow the signs to US 98 west. Take US 98 to County Road 292 and turn south. Cross to Perdido Key. Take County Road 182, running parallel with the Gulf, until you reach the bridge over Perdido Pass. Both contact points of the bridge provide parking, but the western side caters more to the angler.*

The western side of Alabama Point Fishing Park is one of the few spots along the Emerald Coast designed to accommodate anglers. Here a seawall stands along Perdido Pass for several hundred yards, providing anglers an excellent platform for fishing. Cylinders for holding unattended rods also line the wall, enabling anglers to work multiple lines.

Underwater rocks bump up against the western portion of the seawall, and bluefish, mackerel, and drums are hooked using cut baits positioned on the bottom. The mid-section of the platform draws similar quarry, though underwater structures do not come into play. Generally, fish biting in one area of the seawall arrive at the next shortly thereafter. Note that waters in this whole area are cloudy. When fishing with artificial lures, such as spoons or jigs, tip with cut bait to add the necessary scent. Noise-making lures work well, too.

The eastern section of the platform runs under a bridge, so pilings become an added advantage. Snappers and sheepshead are caught here, as well as the above mentioned species. However, this point is slightly farther inland; thus migrating fish sometimes retreat to the Gulf before making it here. Watch the other anglers. If fish are striking on the western side and the eastern side is slow, then move toward the action.

> *Redfish: Spring, late September through November—alewives,
>   blue crabs*
> *Sheepshead: February through March—live shrimp, sand fleas*
> *Spanish Mackerel: April through May, September through
>   November—spoons*
> *Speckled Trout: May, September through December—live
>   shrimp, alewives*
> *Snapper: June through September—squid, shrimp*
> *Pompano: March through May, September to November—jigs*
> *Bluefish: March to November—live bait, jigs*

4) Cotton Bayou and Ono Island

Directions: *From US 331 turn west onto US 98. Pass through Gulf Breeze into Pensacola and onto Gregory Street. Follow the signs to US 98 west. Take US 98 to County Road 292. Turn south on County Road 292 and cross onto Perdido Key. Take County Road 182 to County Road 161 and turn right. Follow the signs to the boat launch at the western end of Cotton Bayou. This launch provides boat access to several inland water areas.*

The waters around Cotton Bayou and Ono Island are teeming with game fish in the spring and fall. Most anglers fish these seasons and leave the summer for the sunbathers. But even in the heat of the summer when nothing else bites speckled trout are in abundance here. That is, if you know about night fishing.

The banks in the Ono Island and Cotton Bayou vicinity are excellent for angling speckled trout at night. From June to September the dark hours provide speckled trout the cooler water they desire. They still need light to feed, however, so taking advantage of boathouse and dock lights is the best way to catch these fish. The key is keeping quiet. Engine rumbling, chatter, or any unnecessary noise should be avoided. Keep silent and you will catch specks with frequency.

Fish during the week instead of the weekends. The low traffic of weekdays builds the fish's confidence. They strike harder and more frequently. Also, the week before the full moon and the week of the new moon are spectacular for night fishing, as specks feed primarily at night during these periods. Live shrimp are the bonny bait providing the action and the scent necessary to draw trout. Be sure to thread them over a long shank hook. Fish them on the bottom, top, or all points in between until you find where they are striking.

> *Redfish: Spring, late September through November—alewives,*
> *blue crabs*
> *Speckled Trout: May, September through December—live*
> *shrimp, alewives*
> *Snapper: June to early September—cut bait, shrimp*

5) Johnson Beach National Seashore
Directions: *From US 331 turn west onto US 98. Pass through Gulf Breeze into Pensacola and onto Gregory Street. Follow the signs to US 98 west. Take US 98 to County Road 292 and turn south. Cross to Perdido Key. Turn left (east) onto Johnson Beach Road and continue into the National Seashore.*

Perdido Key translated from Spanish means lost island, but the only thing to be lost nowadays is in failing to visit this preserve. Although the island's eastern point is not accessible by automobile, the shores to the north and south are premium angling locations. The surfside (south) caters to migrating species like pompano, bluefish, ling, and jacks. These game fish are plentiful on windless mornings, especially when the tide is going out and bait fish are tumbling in the surf. Use the low angle of the morning light to see beyond the surface water. The dark colorings of cobia and bluefish are easily discerned in this manner. After practice, you will notice the lighter hued species, like pompano and flounder.

Points and sloughs jut in and out all along the northern shores of Perdido Key and provide shelter for game fish, which wait here—particularly in Grand Lagoon—to ambush bait fish rounding the points. Thus, retrieving a lure over these areas draws strikes. Species running in the lagoon also cruise the shoreline in search of food. Position shrimp just off the points to lure them. Grass beds pepper this lagoon side, too. To locate these, turn north off the main road and park where a side road dead-ends into the Bay. From there, wade-fish the shoreline using live bait, like shrimp, or mid-water plugs. The best time to fish is at the onset of an outgoing tide, but do not let the shallow waters deter you. Reds and specks will sometimes feed in water just over ankle deep.

Lagoon

> *Redfish: Spring, late September through November—alewives, blue crabs*
> *Speckled Trout: May, September through December—live shrimp, alewives*
> *White trout: Spring, Fall—shrimp, cut bait*

Surfside

> *Jack Crevalle: July and August—finger mullet, jigs*
> *Flounder: October to March—live shrimp, grubs*
> *Pompano: March through May, September to November—jigs*
> *Bluefish: March to November—live bait, jigs*
> *Whiting: March to November—cut bait*
> *Cobia: Late March through April—oversized jigs*

6) Fort Pickens-Gulf Islands National Seashore

Directions: *From US 331 turn west onto US 98. Pass through Fort Walton Beach and turn left over the Navarre Bridge spanning the Santa Rosa Sound. Turn right onto County Road 399 running parallel to the Gulf coastline. Travel west toward Pensacola Beach into Fort Pickens State Park.*

Surf and pier fishing locales hide among the bunkers and fortified walls of Fort Pickens. The entrance fee is minimal and includes
a blanket fishing license, as well as access to the military relics. No
prior license is necessary. As a note, the admission ticket into Fort
Pickens is good for seven days and also includes admittance into
Johnson Beach National Seashores (and vice versa).

Surf fishing for pompano is excellent here. Although pompano
are primarily migratory fish, for unknown reasons they inhabit
these shores year-round. These fish run up and down the shores in
the spring and fall seasons and move into the deeper holes and
sloughs in the wintertime. Sand fleas are the preferred bait in all but
the hottest months when pompano retreat to deeper, cooler waters.

A fishing pier extends toward the pass near the western end of
the fort, and game fish move from the pass to chase bait fish near
shore. Spanish mackerel, jacks, redfish, and sheepshead are hooked
using live shrimp, spoons, and jigs. But be sure to check the bait
fish inhabiting the area. If possible, bait with live specimens of these
or use appropriate artificial lures.

Surfside

Jack Crevalle: July and August—finger mullet, jigs
Flounder: October to March—live shrimp, grubs
Pompano: March through May, September to November—jigs
Bluefish: March to November—live bait, jigs
Whiting: March to November—cut bait
Cobia: Late March through April—oversized jigs

Pier Fishing

Flounder: October to December—cut bait
*Redfish: Spring, late September through November—alewives,
    blue crabs*
Sheepshead: February through March—live shrimp, sand fleas
*Spanish Mackerel: April through May, September through
    November—spoons*
King Mackerel: April to June—live bait fish

7) Three Mile Bridge

Directions: *From US 331 turn west onto US 98. Go through Destin, Fort Walton Beach, and into Gulf Breeze. The Three Mile Bridge fishing bridge is located under the new bridge on the west end of US 98. The Bridge is drive-on style, and you can enter on either the mainland or island side. But note, the middle section was removed to allow the large vessels to pass through, so choose one side or the other. Three Mile Bridge is also referred to as the Gulf Breeze Municipal Fishing Pier.*

Three Mile Bridge provides access to the phenomenal fishing in Pensacola Bay. A fee is charged, but vehicles are allowed on the bridge, thus eliminating the hassle of toting gear. The platform is extremely long and prevents anglers from bumping elbows and tangling lines. This also keeps the competition low and the odds of landing game fish high.

I recommend packing several rods for the wide range of species running through these waters. Sharks, tarpon, and kings are a few of the larger species seen here. Mullet are excellent live bait when lip-hooked and positioned near the surface. Slicing a butterfly bait is an excellent alternative: even though the fish is dead, the loose flanks sway (simulating a live fish) and release oils and fluids that operate like chum.

Redfish are fond of the pilings and rock piles around Three Mile Bridge. Specimens over 10 pounds are landed frequently. Most strike live shrimp and put up an unforgettable fight on light or medium tackle. Many redfish fight for up to thirty minutes and make three or four strong runs before being landed. These strong runs, rather than the acrobatic showmanship of many species, make redfish a most exciting game fish to play.

Note: Locals to this area often refer to blue runners as hardtails.

> **Blue Runner:** *Spring, Fall—jigs, spoons*
> **Redfish:** *Spring, late September through November—alewives, blue crabs*

> *Spanish Mackerel: April through May, September through November—spoons*
> *Speckled Trout: May, September through December—live shrimp, alewives*
> *White Trout: Spring, Fall—shrimp, cut bait*

8) Bob Sikes Bridge

Directions: *From US 331 turn west onto US 98. Go through Destin and Fort Walton Beach and into Gulf Breeze. Turn left and follow the signs to Pensacola Beach. This road will take you over the Bob Sikes Bridge. The structure is accessible from both sides.*

Bob Sikes Bridge, or Old Bay Bridge, spans the Santa Rosa Sound, with the exception of the mid-section that was removed for channel traffic. Parking is available on both sides of the bridge, but drive-on fishing traffic is prohibited. Fishing is also allowed underneath either side of the bridge.

The Old Bay Bridge is a short drive from Three Mile Bridge (Hot Spot 7), but is the better option when fishing for speckled trout. Grass beds are prominent here, and specks are regular catches during season. Gulf specimens of spotted sea trout (as they are called elsewhere in the U.S.) usually feed in schools, and when one is caught subsequent catches follow. Most do not exceed 3 pounds, and 5 pounds is a healthy catch along the Emerald Coast. Wear light-colored clothing and keep noise minimal when fishing speckled (or white) trout. Once you have located them, keep fishing the same spot until they quit hitting. These runs often last for hours.

Make sure to wet your hands before handling these fish. Failing to do so removes the protective oils from their skin and usually results in their death. When keeping trout, pack them on ice immediately after catching. They are excellent table fish but lose their flavor quickly when allowed to warm.

Flounder: October to December—cut bait
Redfish: Spring, late September through November—alewives,
blue crabs
Sheepshead: February through March—live shrimp, sand fleas
Speckled Trout: May, September through December—live
shrimp, alewives

Navarre to Destin (See map next page)

9) National Seashores
Directions: *From US 331 turn west onto US 98 and pass through Fort Walton Beach. Turn left over the Navarre Bridge. Turn right onto US 399. Approximately 10 miles outside Navarre Beach, toward Pensacola Beach, you will enter the National Seashores on Santa Rosa Island. Ample parking is provided, but use the designated areas.*

The National Seashores are some of the most desolate along the Emerald Coast. The competition is almost nonexistent, and the waters are teeming with game fish. However, few conveniences are in the vicinity. Be sure to stock enough food, drink, bait, and tackle to last the day.

Whiting and flounder are hooked using bottom rigs baited with shrimp, sand fleas, or cut baits. Cast the rig beyond the break for whiting, and use a flat-sided sinker to prevent the currents from dragging the bait to shore. When present, whiting are hooked consistently in this manner throughout the day. They are also excellent table fish.

If you desire more action than bottom fishing, then flounder can be lured with artificials. Jigs produce good results and also lure pompano and bluefish in their according seasons. But the best artificial lure for flounder is a grub-tail with a lead head. Use a pink or red tail with a 5/8-ounce white head. Cast beyond the break and allow the grub to sink to the bottom. Use a moderate retrieve and stall about every sixth turn to allow the grub to touch bottom. Combine this with some rod action, and the flounder will follow the lure into the shallow waters. As the bait nears shore, stall it long

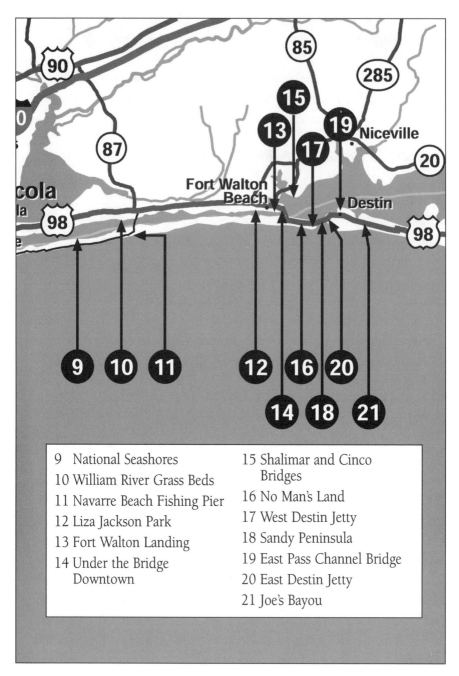

9   National Seashores
10 William River Grass Beds
11 Navarre Beach Fishing Pier
12 Liza Jackson Park
13 Fort Walton Landing
14 Under the Bridge
    Downtown

15 Shalimar and Cinco
    Bridges
16 No Man's Land
17 West Destin Jetty
18 Sandy Peninsula
19 East Pass Channel Bridge
20 East Destin Jetty
21 Joe's Bayou

Navarre to Destin

enough for the flounder to strike. This technique is especially effective during flatter waters when sighting fish is easier.

Days of flatter water also allow fishing from the sand bar. Casting from here accesses deeper waters otherwise unreachable when surf fishing. The morning and evening hours are preferred. The low angle of sunlight helps to discern the schools and pods migrating along the coastline. Bluefish, pompano, and cobia are common catches in their respective seasons.

> *Flounder: October to March—live shrimp, grubs*
> *Pompano: March through May, September to November—jigs*
> *Bluefish: March to November—live bait, jigs*
> *Whiting: March to November—cut bait*
> *Cobia: Late March through April—oversized jigs*

10) William River Grass Beds

Directions: *Take US 98 west from US 331, pass the Navarre Beach Bridge, and head west until you reach the Navarre Beach School Zone. Take a left on Thresher Drive into the Navarre Shores subdivision. At the end of Thresher take a right. After 200 yards the road will turn to red clay. Drive the clay road past the last house, and take the first left (it looks like a trail). Park here.*

The William River Grass Beds are roughly one-half- by one-half-mile in size. Its channels are 20 feet across at their widest and gradually narrow into impassable tributaries the farther inland they travel. At deepest they run about 8 feet. Fishing from a skiff is the best option, although fishing from the banks is excellent, too. Shoes are necessary when fishing from the banks. Working left or right from the parking area accesses plenty of prime waters, but you will have to maneuver over some sketchy ground.

This area is prime for angling trout hiding along the grass beds. The water is dark here so baits with a strong scent, such as live shrimp, are most productive. If you prefer artificial lures, top water plugs that create moderate surface noise, like chuggers, help quarry locate the bait. Remaining quiet is crucial in this particular area. Very little traffic passes through, and the fish are easily spooked. Pole or paddle a skiff through the channels rather than using a trolling motor. Keep talk and other nonessential noise minimal.

Redfish are another prominent species here. Blue crabs and alewives draw them near the grasses. Three-inch crabs fished on the bottom are effective, as are shrimp and cut baits. However, the latter two often draw crabs, which steal baits and cause line inflections that feel similar to red drums testing a bait. Using live bait fish eliminates this nuisance.

> *Redfish: Spring, late September through November—alewives, blue crabs*
> *Speckled Trout: May, September through December—live shrimp, alewives*
> *White trout: April through May, Fall—live shrimp, cut bait*

11) Navarre Beach Fishing Pier
Directions: *From US 331 turn west onto US 98. Pass through Destin and Fort Walton, proceeding approximately 15 miles to the Navarre Bridge, which spans the Santa Rosa Sound. Turn left over the bridge and go south until you reach the first intersection on Santa Rosa Island. Turn right onto County Road 399. The pier is on the immediate left.*

Several years ago the Navarre Beach Fishing Pier endured a hurricane. The end of the pier was lost to the storm, but the remaining structure is intact and safe for fishing. The competition here is high due a shortage of organized angling spots in the area, but this pier has proven one of the most successful over the years.

The Navarre Beach Pier still extends far enough into the Gulf to hook game fish, like king mackerel up to 50 pounds and cobia nearing 100 pounds. These cobia are hooked annually from late March to early May during their spring run. Bait with oversized jigs or pinfish. Kings strike pinfish as well. Spanish mackerel, bluefish, and bonito are other common catches. Spoons or jigs are excellent artificial lures, and finger mullet are excellent bait for all types of pier fishing.

A good tactic for fishing piers is to check out the day-to-day fishing forecasts prior to purchasing bait. The Navarre pier is free so you must work the other anglers for this information. For piers charging a fee, boards are updated each day that highlight baits being used and species being hooked. Use them. They are reliable sources that help eliminate the guesswork. The boards are usually located near the ticket windows.

For more information on fishing piers see Hot Spot 25.

> *Spanish Mackerel: April to June—spoons*
> *Pompano: March through May, September to November—jigs*
> *Bluefish: March to November—live bait, jigs*
> *Cobia: Late March through April—oversized jigs*
> *Bonito: May to September—live bait fish, spoons*

12) Liza Jackson Park
Directions: *From US 331 turn west onto US 98. Pass through Santa Rosa Beach, Destin, and over Brooks Bridge into Fort Walton. Continue on US 98 through Fort Walton for roughly 7 miles. The east entrance to the park is the next left, but continue for one-quarter mile. Turn left into the west entrance. Free parking is available for cars and trailers, and two boat ramps are open for public access.*

Liza Jackson Park is a relief between the strip malls and bistros that clutter US 98. Picnic tables, playgrounds, and shores lined with grass beds provide entertainment for the entire family. Boaters can access the Narrows of the Intracoastal Waterway from the free boat ramps.

For the angler, grass beds are hidden along these banks, particularly heading west toward Navarre Beach. Fish here at high tide (at low tide the water is too shallow) using live shrimp. On calm days surface lures are an excellent substitute. Redfish, speckled trout, and white trout are the most common quarry. Remember to take extra caution when releasing trout. Improper handling can be fatal to these delicate species. Refer to the section on speckled trout for proper releasing techniques.

The park is also equipped with a sizable dock. Live shrimp or cut baits fished on the bottom work well, and sand fleas are excellent when available. Angle the bottom near the pilings for snappers, spadefish, and for smaller specimens of sheepshead common to the area.

> *Redfish:* Spring, late September through November—alewives,
>   blue crabs
> *Speckled Trout:* May, September through December—live
>   shrimp, alewives

13) Fort Walton Landing
Directions: *From US 331 turn west onto US 98. Cross over Brooks Bridge into Fort Walton and turn left at the first traffic light onto Brooks Street. About one-half mile down on the left is the Fort Walton Landing. A boat launch is provided, but parking is somewhat limited.*

Fort Walton Landing is similar to Liza Jackson Park in angling value but is less populated by anglers, thus less competitive. A boardwalk extends east to west along the shoreline, and numerous pilings occupy the immediate waters. The boat launch provides access to the Narrows.

Red drums forage along the oyster beds located just beyond the pilings. Blue crabs with their shells removed are effective bait. Allow the redfish to nibble the meat from the shell before attempting to set the hook. Disregard the gentle inflections in the line and set the hook only when you feel a steady surge. Shrimp are another good bait but are easily picked away by crabs and bait fish. For better protection thread shrimp over a long shank hook.

A grass bed is located at the eastern end of the landing and is easily reachable by casting from shore. Trout and redfish wait next to the beds to ambush prey and to avoid becoming someone else's. Trout generally bump a bait two or three times then run with it. Do not yank back to set the hook. Steady tension is plenty and anything more rips the barb from their soft mouths.

> *Redfish: Spring, late September through November—alewives,*
> *blue crabs*
> *Speckled Trout: May, September through December—live*
> *shrimp, alewives*

14) Under the Bridge Downtown
Directions: *From US 331 head west on US 98 over the Destin Bridge until you reach the base of Brooks Bridge in Fort Walton Beach. On each side, a semicircular access road loops under the connecting point of land and bridge. Parking is available at both locations.*

Brooks Bridge spans the Intracoastal Waterway, and as a general rule fishing is prohibited from structures that span the Waterway. However, fishing is allowed from the concrete land-bound bases as long as your line does not enter the channel. Thus, angling is legal from both sides underneath the Brooks Bridge.

Fish here in the early morning hours during a rising tide. Bluerunners, crevalles, and pompano school through the area in their respective seasons, and angling is best before the Waterway traffic arrives. Alewives and other bait fish linger around the pilings in large schools and draw feeding game fish. As a rule, always mimic the local bait fish for the best results. Use alewives for bait if possible. Re-bait when necessary (if the original looks sluggish or dies) to maintain the desired visual action. Also note that alewives are preferred by most species along the Emerald Coast.

Sheepshead, snappers, and spadefish also frequent the area at various times of year. Sand fleas draw the most strikes but often are difficult to come by. Shrimp are good alternatives. Fish at various depths along the pilings. The idea here, especially for sheepshead, is to intermingle your bait with the cloudy chum that occurs as these game fish scrape barnacles from the pilings. Another method is to use a basic bottom rig. Position it against the underwater boulders about 10 feet from the embankment. Use live or cut baits to add scent to the visual lure.

> *Sheepshead: February through March—live shrimp, sand fleas*
> *Spanish Mackerel: April through May, September through*
> *November—spoons*
> *Snapper: June through September—cut bait, shrimp*
> *Spadefish: Late June to August—live shrimp, sand fleas*
> *Jack Crevalle: July and August—finger mullet, jigs*

15) Shalimar and Cinco Bridges
Directions: *From US 331 turn west onto US 98. Pass over the Destin Bridge and the Fort Walton Bridge and slow at the first traffic light. Turn right at Cash's Liquor and go north about 1 1/2 miles, then merge right onto County Road 85. The first bridge you reach is Cinco. The second is Shalimar.*

Fishing the Cinco and Shalimar Bridges is similar to angling Brooks Bridge (Hot Spot 14) but with a few advantages. Competition is lower because they are farther off the beaten path and not commonly known. Also, certain species travel the extra distance upstream to forage and spawn in the less salty waters. Thus, these venues are excellent alternatives when angling downstream is overcrowded or slow.

Local fishermen produce the most catches by working all three bridges in a single day. They move from bridge to bridge, by automobile or boat, as the tides rise and fall. For example, they begin the day by fishing the start of a falling tide at one bridge. Then they move down to catch the prime times at subsequent bridges. Use a tide chart to determine when to begin, and move up or downstream accordingly. Better yet, tag along with a local when possible.

Angling techniques and species for fishing these spots are highlighted in Hot Spot 14.

> *Redfish: Spring, late September through November—alewives, blue crabs*
> *Sheepshead: February through March—live shrimp, sand fleas*
> *Snapper: June through September—cut bait, shrimp*
> *Spadefish: Late June to August—live shrimp, sand fleas*
> *Jack Crevalle: July and August—finger mullet, jigs*

16) No Man's Land

Directions: *From US 331 take US 98 west through Destin and cross over the Destin Bridge. On the left, spanning between Destin and Fort Walton, is a stretch of beach. Parking is available at the proper beach access points scattered along the stretch.*

Fishing the vacant beaches between Destin and Fort Walton is legal, although the military signs posted have acted as a false deterrent to the public. The signs state simply not to drive on the beaches, so curb your auto at an access point and trek to the shores. Very few people fish here so the surf fishing is excellent due to a lack of competition for miles.

Pompano, bluefish, and jacks school along these shores. In spring and autumn they appear as large shadows moving parallel to the coastline, usually between the first and second sand bar. Wade out and fish from the first sand bar if schools are running farther out. A jig with pink, red, and white coloring is the best artificial lure and eliminates the trouble of re-baiting with natural baits when the schools are moving by and time is precious. Cast over and in front of the school and use a swift retrieve. On calm days, wading deep enough to spot-fish cobia is possible. Look for two to four large shadows moving together—cobia usually travel in pairs or pods. Bait with an oversized jig.

Keep in mind where you store your bounty while fishing from the sand bar. Fish strung on a line and tied around the waist prove convenient for the angler, but also for larger game fish seeking food in the area. Often blood is drawn while removing the hook from a fish's mouth. This acts as chum, and sharks are a main concern. Prevent this by keeping your catches in a cooler on the beach.

> *Jack Crevalle: July and August—finger mullet, jigs*
> *Pompano: March through May, September to November—jigs*
> *Bluefish: March to November—live bait, jigs*
> *Cobia: Late March through April—oversized jigs*

17) West Destin Jetty

Directions: *From US 331 take US 98 west through Destin, pass over the East Channel Pass Bridge (Destin Bridge), and on the far side of the bridge take an immediate left onto the gravel road. Parking is plentiful.*

Wading waters and the West Destin Jetty waters are accessible at this Hot Spot. For wade fishing, start under the Destin Bridge (the water is knee to waist deep) and work north along the shoreline. Angle along the grass beds with live shrimp to draw specks, redfish, and species chasing bait fish toward the banks. Follow the shoreline south to the West Destin Jetty to fish the surf or pass. Pack lightly and plan to get wet. Gulf waves often shower those who venture out, especially during high tide.

Fishing is productive from the sides and the ends of jetties. However, angling the jetty end lends itself to large specimens of cobia, jacks, and mackerel and justifies the longer trek and higher competition. Early spring is prime time for spot fishing cobia, and jetties and piers are the only two platforms allowing land-based fisherman a shot at them. Oversized jigs, or boathead lures (as they are called along the Emerald Coast), are the bonny bait. But throwing a boathead lure all day is tiring. Rig two poles before going cobia fishing. Use a medium or heavy rig only when cobia are spotted. Use the second, lighter rig, to fish the other species. King and Spanish mackerel are taken during late spring on bait fish and large surface lures. Cast directly off the point in order to reach the farthest offshore waters possible. Use a wire leader for kings to inhibit their razor teeth. A wire leader is also suggested for the Spanish mackerel.

Techniques for fishing the sides of jetties are discussed in Hot Spot 20.

> **Spanish Mackerel:** *April through May, September through*
> *November—spoons*
> **Ladyfish:** *June to September—shiny spoons, jigs*
> **Pompano:** *March through May, September to November—jigs*
> **Bluefish:** *March to November—live bait, jigs*

18) Sandy Peninsula

Directions: *Take US 98 west from US 331. Enter Destin city limits and turn left onto Gulf Shore Drive. This road ends at a sandy parking lot with ample parking.*

A peninsula of beach starts from this parking lot, runs down the harbor to the East Pass channel, and returns along the lively waters nearer the Gulf. On the peninsula's southern side the sand is eroded so that the embankment rises 10 feet above sea level. This perch is prime for spot fishing, and the waters are deep enough to draw big game. Cast from the embankment using live bait or artificial lures, like jigs or spoons. But note, a high perch alters the action of an artificial lure during retrieve. Flounder and white trout strike cut baits here, as do Spanish mackerel and bluefish cruising around the point before heading into the Bay.

Sea oat restoration is in progress at the point, but skirting the coastline accesses the fish swimming the East Pass Channel waters. Live bait fish hooked through the lip and drifted in the currents lure drums, sharks, and other species running the channel. However, boat traffic is high in the channel at times so stick to the harbor-side shore during the peak seasons. Boat dock pilings are within casting distance. Fishing with shrimp is preferred but often draws unwanted species, such as pinfish. Use them for cut bait and fish through until the game fish arrive. Red and black drums and trout inhabit these waters, and migrating species move through the area in the fall and spring.

> **Redfish:** *Spring, late September through November—alewives, blue crabs*
>
> **Spanish Mackerel:** *April through May, September through November—spoons*
>
> **White Trout:** *May, September through December—live shrimp, alewives*
>
> **Pompano:** *March through May, September to November—jigs*
>
> **Bluefish:** *March to November—live bait, jigs*

19) East Pass Channel Bridge

Directions: *(to the east side): From US 331 take US 98 west through Destin, and turn left into the Fat Tuesday parking lot before crossing over the Destin Bridge. Park in this vicinity. Fishing is down the embankment toward the bridge.*

A seawall begins to the left of the bridge and continues for 100 feet, providing the angler solid footing and a suitable place to stow gear. The waters are consistently deep and all positions on the wall are equally prosperous. Fishing under the bridge is more difficult due to rock and other debris littering the vicinity. Leave surplus tackle on the seawall and carry only necessary tackle. Once settled here, note the structures and darker waters to identify the most lucrative spots.

Both locals lure the same species. Sheepshead, spadefish, and snappers linger along the wall and around the pilings. Drift sand fleas or live shrimp in the mid-waters and let the currents provide the action. Fishing these baits just off the bottom works well, too, but bait fish steal the shrimp more rapidly when fished at these depths. Redfish are also present near the bottom. Bait with blue crabs or live shrimp and do not set the hook on the first nibbles. Wait until you feel the drum's steady pull, then set the hook firmly.

These waters can also be fished from the catwalk on the bridge. The walk is accessible from both shores so you can park on either side for access. The above species apply here, but use the high vantage to spot schools and pods running the pass. Fish live baits. As a rule, always pack several lures and rigs when fishing around underwater structures, as you will likely lose some of your tackle to entanglements.

> *Redfish: Spring, late September through November—alewives,*
> *   blue crabs*
> *Sheepshead: February through March—live shrimp, sand fleas*
> *Spadefish: June to August—live shrimp, sand fleas*
> *Bluefish: September to November—live bait, cut bait*
> *Snapper: June through September—cut bait, shrimp*

20) East Destin Jetty

Directions: *From US 331 head west on US 98 into the Destin city limits. Turn left onto Gulf Shore Drive and go approximately 3 to 4 miles. Just after Poolside Villas, look for a small blue and white sign on your left signifying public access to the beach. The right shoulder directly across from the sign provides limited public parking with room for only ten to fifteen automobiles. Walk through the public access and out to the jetty (about a $^1/_4$-mile walk).*

The East Destin Jetty enables angling in the deeper waters outside the second sand bar, as well as at the mouth of the East Channel Pass. The hike to both areas is rather grueling, and maneuvering along the jetty is daunting with gear in hand. Pack light, but prepare for game fish small and large.

Fishing on the inlet side is best for hooking the smaller species, such as Spanish mackerel, bluefish and pompano. The bottom drops away rapidly here so casting a bait into the deep waters is easy. Fish cut baits on the bottom for the hard-striking bluefish that, pound for pound, are one of the most spectacular fighters in the Gulf. A wire leader is required. Shrimp, live or dead, also lure blue-fish, plus pompano, sailcats, and jacks. Use a heavy monofilament leader, 14- to 20-pound test, 10 feet long, unless you are fishing particularly for pompano (in which case use no leader). Fighting and landing fish at the jetties often results in your line abrading against the rocks, and a leader helps prevent losing a fish to weakened line.

Techniques for fishing the end of this jetty are discussed in Hot Spot 17.

> *Jack Crevalle: July and August—finger mullet, jigs*
> *Spanish Mackerel: April to June—spoons*
> *Pompano: March through May, September to November—jigs*
> *Bluefish: March to November—live bait, jigs*

21) Joe's Bayou
Directions: *From US 331 go west on US 98 through Destin. Take the last right (before crossing the Destin Bridge) onto Calhoun Avenue. Continue until Calhoun changes to Silbert Avenue and then to First Street. The road comes to a dead end at Joe's Bayou Boat Ramp. Parking and two boat ramps are provided at no fee. Two additional launches are forthcoming.*

Fishing is prohibited directly in front of the boat ramps, but wade fishing is excellent if you work along the banks to the left. The Bayou begins to open into the Bay and the fish run through this mouth. Grass beds line the banks, providing excellent shelter for foraging speckled trout and redfish. Follow the shoreline around for several hundred yards. The water remains knee to waist deep.

A common rule carries over for all types of fishing. If you want to catch bigger fish, you've got to use bigger bait. Large specimens are not likely to hit a 2-inch ronker. Such a small meal is not worth their time or energy. Fish want one large meal in order to return to cover quickly, thus lessening their chances of becoming dinner to a predator higher on the food chain.

Upping the size of your bait fish entices bigger game. Baiting with a 5- to 8-inch artificial lure draws the bigger species along the Emerald Coast. However, the number of catches decreases since fewer big ones exist.

> *Redfish: Spring, late September through November—alewives, blue crabs*
>
> *Speckled Trout: May, September through December—live shrimp, artificial lures*

22) Stallworth Lake

Directions: *From US 331 turn west onto US 98 and continue to the west entrance of Scenic County Road 30-A. Turn left and go approximately 3 miles until the road corners left and begins running parallel with the Gulf. At this bend turn right onto Highland Avenue. Park on the brick cul-de-sac where Highland ends. Use the boardwalk for public access to the beach. Once on the beach, turn right and follow the shoreline for 300 yards. On your right is a channel that leads to Stallworth Lake.*

At high tide, the channel feeding Stallworth Lake opens a pass for fish of all species. This lake, like others in the area, stocks ronkers, barracuda, and everything in between. The canal runs for about 100 yards, and despite its narrowness is 4 to 5 feet deep in some places. Where the canal stops, the lake dives deep, creating a wall for fish to forage. The long stretches of shoreline on either side of the channel provide access for fishing. As in all areas, stay off the dunes and help preserve the surroundings.

Fishing along the shoreline works best for hooking specks and redfish. A top-water artificial retrieved at a moderate pace churns the surface enough to attract fish in these otherwise calm waters. Live shrimp are excellent bait as well. Avoid noisy lures that spook specks.

Fishing the deeper waters from shore also achieves results. This lake floor falls away just off the shoreline, and enables you to reach depths not often obtainable when fishing from shore. An easy cast gets you into water 20 feet deep. Shrimp or cut baits are the most versatile option for bottom fishing. Predicting exactly what game fish will be here at any given time is impossible (see Hot Spot 25), but cut baits prove most effective overall. On the other hand, if you are interested in trying to hook a jack or barracuda, stick with a pink-and-white or red-and-white jig, and use a swift retrieve to draw these speedy game fish.

> *Redfish: Spring and Fall—blue crabs, artificial lures*
> *Speckled Trout: Spring and Fall—plugs*
> *Black Drum: September through December—plugs, live bait fish*
> *Flounder: October through February—cut bait*

23) Hogtown Bayou

Directions: *From US 331 turn west onto US 98. Go approximately 3 miles to the intersection of County Road 393, and take a right. Hogtown Bayou is 2 miles north on the left.*

Locally referred to as Hogtown Landing, Cessa Landing has ample parking for automobiles and boat trailers and offers two free boat launches for accessing the other waters of the Choctawhatchee Bay. Restroom facilities and picnic areas are open to the public.

Grass beds lace the immediate waters of this bayou, and the shallows leading up to them provide excellent wade and shore fishing to the angler on foot. Redfish and specks are commonly caught at the Landing, although I suggest wading westward along the southern bank of the bayou to increase your odds. (As a rule, your chances of catching fish are better the farther away you travel from the competition and commotion—in this case, away from the boat ramps and picnics.)

The grass beds become more plentiful as you move westward. Finger mullet and ronkers stock the shallows and entice wary game.

Net your own bait fish here, as specimens are plentiful. Remember, baiting with a species common to the area usually works best. Blue crabs can be found near the edge of the grass beds too. Remove the top shell, bait, and use the scent to draw redfish. Hooking large trout from these grasses is also common. Bait with resident bait fish or live shrimp. Snappers and sailcats are caught occasionally in the shallows, but you need a boat to hook the biggest species in the open water.

Outside the bayou the water opens into the Choctawhatchee Bay. The angling spots become endless using a skiff. As in all bays along the Emerald Coast, grass beds prosper. Motoring along the shores is the best way to find the sloughs housing the game fish. Also look for small canals that appear to run dry just inland. Often these narrow passes wind around and open up into lakes hidden behind the walls of grass. The larger trout and redfish reside in these less accessible and less obvious places.

> *Redfish: Late September through November—alewives*
> *Speckled Trout: Spring, September to January—live shrimp*
> *White Trout: Spring, September to December—live shrimp*

HOT SPOTS EAST OF US 331

Seaside to Panama City (see map opposite)

24) Old US 331 Bridge

Directions: *Heading south on US 331, pass over the bridge spanning Choctawhatchee Bay. On this southern side of the bridge is Mangos, a bar and restaurant. Parking is available under the bridge.*

The Old US 331 Bridge may no longer be suitable for traffic of the automobile variety, but it provides an excellent platform for anglers working the Choctawhatchee Bay. The middle section of the bridge was removed to provide passage for larger vessels sailing the channel, but fishermen can still access the remaining portions from the northern and southern ends. Ample parking is provided underneath it on both sides, and the walk to the bridge is minimal. I recommend accessing the southern side. The bar and restaurant located here, Mangos, is home to many local fishermen. Hang around and you are bound to find out exactly what is biting and on what baits.

Fish feeding off structures as well as bottom dwellers frequent the waters here. Toward the end of the bridge sheepshead linger at various depths while foraging barnacles off the pilings. Combine sand fleas with patience to land these finicky fish. Oyster beds also account for a number of bottom dwellers in the area. Fishing under the bridge along the western banks is the best chance at hooking them. The beds are located within casting distance directly off shore, and blue crabs, prime bait for luring red and black drums, can be netted from the shoreline rocks underfoot. Spanish mackerel also show around the bridge during their migratory seasons. They travel in large schools and when one is hooked in an area usually everyone catches their limit. Fish silver or gold spoons with a moderate retrieve.

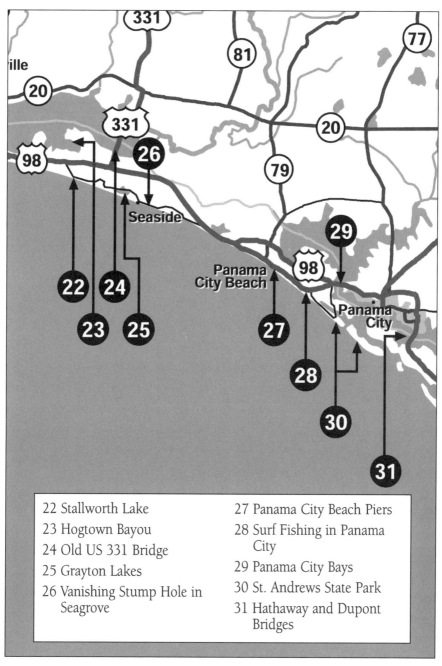

22 Stallworth Lake
23 Hogtown Bayou
24 Old US 331 Bridge
25 Grayton Lakes
26 Vanishing Stump Hole in Seagrove

27 Panama City Beach Piers
28 Surf Fishing in Panama City
29 Panama City Bays
30 St. Andrews State Park
31 Hathaway and Dupont Bridges

Seaside to Panama City

>*Flounder:* October to December—cut bait
>*Redfish:* Spring, late September through November—alewives,
> blue crabs
>*Sheepshead:* February through March—live shrimp, sand fleas
>*Spanish Mackerel:* April through May, September through
> November—spoons
>*Speckled Trout:* May, September through December—live
> shrimp, alewives

25) Grayton Lakes

Directions: *From US 331 turn west onto US 98. Go to County Road 83 and turn left, following the signs to Blue Mountain Beach. County Road 83 comes to a dead end at County Road 30-A. Take a left. The first lake is Big Redfish Lake. The last is Camp Creek Lake. There are several others in between including Little Redfish, Alligator, Western, Eastern, and Deer. These are saltwater or brackish lakes and are accessible to the barefoot fisherman. Most are equipped with boat launches. (Jet-propelled watercrafts are prohibited.)*

The many lakes in the Grayton area provide spectacular fishing along the Emerald Coast. While each lake is unique in species and landscape, a few basic principles can be applied to them collectively. The grass beds lining the lakes' shores are stocked with speckled trout and redfish waiting to ambush bait fish and blue crabs. Positioning a bait, such as live shrimp, along the grass beds draws the quarry out of hiding. Gigging at night is another excellent way of fishing these shallower waters near shore. Flounder and black drums are the typical quarry when gigging.

The lakes' deeper waters lend themselves to a wider variety of game fish. Angling with jigs, plugs, and alewives draws barracuda to drums. However, due to inevitable weather patterns, predicting what species will inhabit these waters from year to year is difficult.

Hurricanes play a significant role in determining what fish fill the lakes in this area. These storms rearrange the shores by redistributing sands and giving the coastline new shape. Sometimes the inlets that allow the Gulf waters to feed the lakes become closed off, prohibiting new fish species from being introduced and resident species from exiting. Some fish cannot survive without the high concentration of salt and die off quickly. But tarpon, for example, can thrive in lakes without a high salt content. Specimens nearing the 100-pound mark have been pulled from lakes years after being closed off from the Gulf. Hurricanes also carve new inlets allowing saltwater to pass into once brackish or freshwater lakes. These newly formed saltwater lakes can then support many species of saltwater game fish. Thus, the fish inhabiting lakes can change on a yearly basis. Predicting what fish will bite from year to year becomes a matter of trial and error. Redfish, flounder, and trout are fairly consistent. For the rest, rig up and see what takes the bait.

> *Flounder: October to December—cut bait*
> *Redfish: September through November—alewives, blue crabs*
> *Speckled Trout: September through December—live shrimp*
> *Black Drum: September through December—live bait*

26) Vanishing Stump Hole in Seagrove
Directions: *From US 331 turn east onto US 98. Take US 98 to the east entrance of Scenic 30-A and turn right. As you enter Seagrove look for public access to Pelayo Beach on your left. Keep your eyes peeled because the sign is hidden. The beach access runs alongside the east edge of a subdivision call Jasmine Dunes.*

Seagrove is home to a stretch of beach that reveals underwater structures when autumn rolls in along the Emerald Coast. The receding tide draws layers of sand to the deep waters, altering the ocean floor. By November dozens of once-concealed tree stumps pepper the shallow waters and extend past the first sand bar. Late-migrating species are attracted to this area where bait fish abound, and fishing remains excellent through December. The venue is one of the few offering the angler a chance to thwart the winter doldrums.

Late-running pompano and bluefish feed here before making their final run down the coastline. Jigs, sand fleas, and dead or live shrimp prove tempting. Also prevalent are resident fish still inhabiting the surf before the real cold arrives. Flounder forage amidst these tree stumps in late autumn before seeking shelter from the cold. Lure these flatfish with cut baits fished on the bottom or with artificial lures jigged along the bottom using a slow retrieve. The pink-and-white grubs with ⅝-ounce lead heads prove very effective.

Refer to Hot Spot 39 for tips on fishing the Vanishing Stump Hole during the high seasons.

> *Flounder: October to March—live shrimp, grubs*
> *Pompano: March through May, September to November—jigs*
> *Bluefish: March to November—live bait*
> *Whiting: March to November—live bait*
> *Cobia: Late March through April—oversized jigs*

27) Two Panama City Beach Piers

Directions: *Take US 98 east from US 331. Turn right off US 98 toward the beachfront road as you enter the Sunnyside Area. Head east along the coast. The first fishing pier is the Panama City Beach Pier (Dan Russell City Pier). Farther east is the County Pier.*

The piers in Panama City Beach provide access to a wide variety of game fish. A blanket permit is included in the fee to fish the Panama City Beach Pier. No prior license is required. On the other hand, County Pier is free, so a Florida fishing license is necessary.

The serious sports fishermen angle the deep waters at the end of the pier. Cobia are common catches here during their spring run. Using an oversized jig tipped with cut bait is a proven method. King and Spanish mackerel are other favorites when fishing these deeper waters. Live bait fish, like pinfish, are the preferred bait. Hook the bait fish on its back (between the tail and dorsal fin) and float it on the surface. It will swim down and away, providing the movement and surface disturbance necessary to attract the larger game. Spanish mackerel in the 2- to 5-pound category are common, and kings up to 100 pounds are landed periodically. Competition at the end of the pier is high. The crowds can be overbearing. The more leisurely angler has other options.

Fishing off the pier between the first and second sand bars is just as prosperous and much less competitive. Pompano, bluefish, sailcats, and sheepshead are frequently caught here. Sand fleas prove most effective, and are fished on the surface, at various depths, or on the bottom. Schooling pompano and bluefish strike them anywhere. Sailcats take them off the bottom. And, from time to time, sheepshead hit them when positioned in the mid-waters near the pilings. Squid and shrimp are effective alternatives, and jigs are the best artificial lures. However, stick to sand fleas when fishing for sheepshead.

> *King Mackerel: July to September—live bait fish*
> *Cobia: March through April—oversized jigs*
> *Spanish Mackerel: April to June—shiny lures*
> *Pompano: September through October—jigs*
> *Bluefish: September through October—artificial lures*

28) Surf Fishing in Panama City

Directions: *From US 331 turn east onto US 98. Turn south toward the Gulf of Mexico in the Laguna Beach vicinity. From here to the St. Andrew State Park the coast is excellent for surf fishing.*

Knowing how to read the water is the key to catching fish consistently in the surf. I have highlighted this particular stretch as a prime example of what to look for when choosing a surf fishing location.

The sand bars in the Panama City Beach area were rearranged when Hurricane Opal blew through in 1996. The sand bar formations shifted into an irregular pattern ideal for drawing quarry to the inshore waters. Now, roughly every 50 feet, breaks occur in the sand bar formation. These breaks cause tidal rips, which are seen as irregularities in the typical parallel wave break. The waves still crash in typical fashion across the shallower waters, but over the breaks, where the water is deeper, the water stays flat.

These pools, or washouts, draw both migratory and stationary species. The stationary fish linger during an entire tidal cycle, whereas the migratory fish run through the washouts, down the sloughs, and exit at another bar break farther down the coast. Pompano and bluefish are the most common quarry running here. Pink-and-white jigs in the 3/4-ounce range are effective, especially when schools pass through during their spring and fall runs. Use a rapid retrieve to keep the jig moving swiftly and off the bottom, and periodically bump the rod tip to enhance its visual effectiveness.

Other species, like flounder and whiting, are more stationary. Bottom fishing with squid or freshly dead shrimp is recommended. Cast just beyond the wave break and let the bait sink to the bottom. This technique also draws the bluefish and pompano, but stick with the jig if you are fishing for those two in particular.

> *Pompano: March through May, September to November—jigs*
> *Bluefish: March to November—live bait, jigs*
> *Whiting: March to November—cut bait*
> *Cobia: Late March through April—oversized jigs*
> *Jack Crevalle: July and August—finger mullet, jigs*

29) Panama City Bays

Directions: *From US 331 turn east onto US 98. A public boat launch is accessible on both sides of Hathaway Bridge: Panama City Marina on the east side, St. Andrew's Yacht Club on the west. From here the West, North, East, and St. Andrew Bays are accessible by small watercraft.*

Six major bays and numerous sounds, bayous, and passes break up the Emerald Coast. Owning a small vessel opens up prime angling spots otherwise unreachable by foot. The Panama City Bays are used here as an example. The following tips apply when angling any of the major inland waters.

Most tackle shops carry maps highlighting the grass beds, shelves, and passes of their local bays, and angling them is best split into those three categories. Fish the grass beds for redfish and trout using live baits. Blue crabs are excellent for redfish and alewives for trout. Live shrimp lure both species. Casting the bait about 3 feet from the grass/water line is the best way to locate these species.

Fishing the shelves is a second option. To begin, locate where the yellowish waters abruptly turn darker. This is the shelf edge or, rather, where the flats fall to deeper waters. Jigs retrieved along this shelf edge provide good results for the faster species, like jacks and mackerel. Bottom fishing with cut bait is also effective, but you will likely hook a few sailcats or stingrays in the process. Fish through them until a more preferable species shows. Everything from sharks to pompano to chicken dolphin are hooked in these open waters.

The inlets make up a third catagory. Fish frequently move in and out of the passes according to the tides, weather, and location of the bait fish. Hook bullreds, crevalles, and other large Gulf Coast game fish from your boat, as you drift along the pass, by positioning bait fish at various depths. Choosing a depth is a matter of knowing what is running at a particular time of year. Ask the locals. If redfish are running, a bait set just off the bottom is most effective. Crevalles and mackerel prefer a bait closer to the surface. Trial and error is the best device. Keep varying the depth until you find where they are hitting.

> *Redfish: October through November—live bait fish*
> *Speckled Trout: Late March through May, Fall—assorted*
> *artificial lures*
> *Snapper: December through February—cut bait*
> *Spanish Mackerel: Late March through May—spoons, shiny*
> *artificial lures*
> *Sheepshead: Early February through March—live shrimp*

30) St. Andrew State Park

Directions: *Take US 98 east from US 331. Turn right onto Thomas Drive, and continue until you enter the State Park.*

St. Andrew State Park provides access to several types of fishing. A dock for angling Grand Lagoon is located on the park's northern side. Speckled trout and redfish are the most likely quarry here. Blue crabs positioned on the bottom near the shoreline grasses lure redfish. Live shrimp, either positioned on the bottom or suspended 2 feet below the surface (using a float) draw specks and redfish. Due to high traffic in this lagoon, fishing is best during the weekdays. Also, note that speckled trout are off limits here during February.

The southeastern tip of the park is fortified with a jetty. Fishing from here enables anglers to reach game running the deep waters of St. Andrew Pass. Pompano, bluefish, and large game fish, like bullreds, are common catches here, especially during the spring and fall migrations. A second jetty is located across the St. Andrew Pass on Shell Island. However, Florida residents need to be aware that although your residency negates the need for a license when land-based fishing, you must have a license to surf fish off Shell Island because a boat is required to reach it. Proper bait and angling techniques for the above species are discussed in the species section of this book.

The park also provides surfside pier fishing. Refer to Hot Spot 27, "Two Panama City Beach Piers," for the particulars on the angling piers in this area.

Gulf side:

Bluefish: September through November—jigs
Spanish Mackerel: April to June—spoons
Tarpon: August through September—spoons, live pinfish
Pompano: September to late October—jigs
King Mackerel: July to September—live bait fish
Cobia: March through April—oversized jigs
Spanish Mackerel: April to June—shiny lures

Lagoon:

*Speckled Trout: Spring, September through November—
assorted artificial lures*

*Redfish: Spring, September through November—live shrimp,
blue crabs*

31) Hathaway and Dupont Bridges

Directions: *Turn east off US 331 onto US 98. Take US 98 to Hathaway
Bridge. To reach the Dupont Bridge continue east on US 98 through
Panama City until you arrive at the next structure spanning the
Intracoastal Waterway.*

The waters around the Hathaway Bridge remain as clear and
emerald as any in the world. This clarity lends itself to spot fishing
around the grass beds. Wading for specks and red drums is excellent in all but the hottest and coldest months. If you prefer to stay
dry, the Panama City Marina, on the east side of the bridge, allows
fishing from designated docks.

Blue crabs and live shrimp placed near the water/grass line provide excellent live baits. For artificial baits avoid noisy and top-
water designs. This water is usually clear enough to tempt the fish's
visual senses, and rattlers and surface lures are too aggressive and
tend to spook the quarry. Occasionally, offshore storms cloud the
water and make noisy lures more effective, but the quiet artificial
lures that retrieve through the mid-waters are the best overall.

When fishing here, also be aware of your own visual and verbal
noise. These fish are sensitive and too much talking or even flashy
garments are enough to scare them away. Dress in light-colored
clothes and keep the chit-chat minimal.

The Old Dupont Bridge is another excellent angling spot in the
Panama City area. The middle section was removed to allow passage to the Intracoastal traffic, and it now caters to anglers. A fee is
charged, and it is walkout only—no automobile traffic is allowed.
Thus, all gear must be toted. Mackerel, sheepshead, flounder, trout,

and redfish are common catches. Live shrimp or cut bait fished deep attracts the drums and other bottom feeders. Suspending a bait in the mid-waters draws mackerel, jacks, and other quarry running under the bridge.

> **Flounder:** *October to December—cut bait*
> **Redfish:** *Spring, late September through November—alewives, blue crabs*
> **Speckled Trout:** *May, September through December—live shrimp, alewives*
> **White Trout:** *Spring, September through November—live shrimp*
> **Sheepshead:** *February through March—live shrimp, sand fleas*
> **Spanish Mackerel:** *April through May, September through November—spoons*

Extra: Heading east on US 98 you arrive at Mexico Beach. Turn right onto 37th Street. This free fishing pier extends into some of the best shark fishing waters along the Gulf.

Port St. Joe to St. George Island (see map opposite)

32) St. Joseph Peninsula State Park

Directions: *From US 331 turn east onto US 98. Pass through Panama City, Mexico Beach, and at the eastern side of Port St. Joe take a right onto County Road 30 (C-30 E). Take County Road 30 through Simmon's Bayou for approximately 4 miles. Turn right onto Cape San Blas Road (following the signs to St. Joseph's State Park) and into the State Park. The cape narrows just past the marina. A boardwalk accesses the surf on the left, and the bay is reachable to the right.*

St. Joseph State Park is 2,500 preserved acres along Cape San Blas. Both bay and gulf waters are accessible here, and the competition is minimal. Cabins, campsites, and picnic areas alongside waters teeming with game fish make up this premier angling spot along the Emerald Coast.

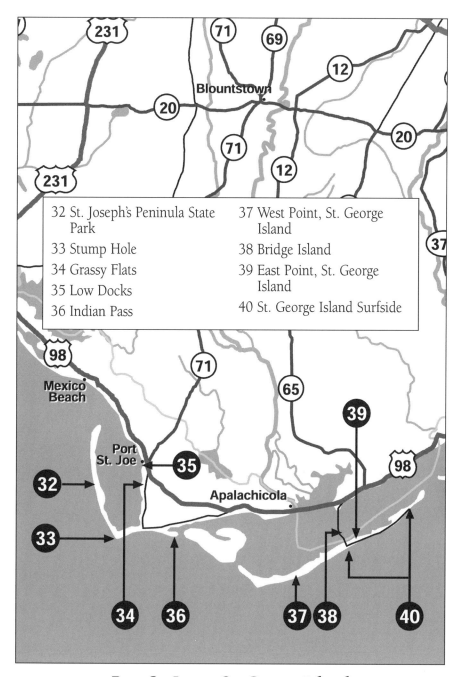

32 St. Joseph's Peninula State Park

33 Stump Hole

34 Grassy Flats

35 Low Docks

36 Indian Pass

37 West Point, St. George Island

38 Bridge Island

39 East Point, St. George Island

40 St. George Island Surfside

Port St. Joe to St. George Island

The bayside shores are lined with grass beds that provide refuge for white and speckled trout. Wading or poling a skiff 20 to 30 feet off the shoreline are ideal tactics for working this area. The last two hours of an ebbing tide are great for angling because game fish feel the urgency to feed before the bait fish recede with the tide. Threading a live shrimp over a long shank hook and positioning the bait 2 to 3 feet off the grasses draws strikes. The specks landed in this area are usually of legal limit and some of the largest specimens caught along the Emerald Coast. Redfish can be fished in the same manner as trout, and if shrimp fail, blue crabs and alewives are alternative baits.

Fishing the flats on the bay side is a second option. The flats extend far from shore and provide a large arena for wade fishing. Spot fishing from a boat is another effective technique when the water is clear. The Grassy Flats Hot Spot highlights the bait and angling techniques for fishing the shallows.

The Gulf side is optimal angling territory during the spring and fall migratory runs. Species running north and west in the spring pass through here prior to being taunted by every other angler along the Emerald Coast. They are more naive and less wary to tactics and take bait frequently and aggressively. Pompano, bluefish, jacks, and king and Spanish mackerel strike here. On calm days, wade out and fish from the first sand bar. A healthy cast can place your bait in the alley, between the first and second sand bars, where migrating fish most often run. Retrieve jigs rapidly to lure these faster species, and stick with bright colors; pompano, in particular, hunt as much by site as by smell. By the same theory, keep terminal tackle minimal to avoid spooking possible catches.

Bay side

Redfish: Spring, late September through November—alewives, blue crabs

Speckled Trout: May, September through December—live shrimp, artificial lures

Gulf side

> **Flounder:** *October to March—live shrimp, grubs*
> **Pompano:** *March through May, September to November—jigs*
> **Bluefish:** *March to November—live bait, jigs*
> **Whiting:** *March to November—live bait*

33) Stump Hole

Directions: *From US 331 turn east onto US 98. Pass through Panama City, Mexico Beach, and at the eastern side of Port St. Joe take a right onto County Road 30 (C-30 E). Take County Road 30 through Simmon's Bayou for approximately 4 miles. Turn right onto Cape San Blas Road (following the signs to St. Joseph's State Park). Continue until you see a long piece of granite on the left side of the road. There is ample parking on the right shoulder. Over the embankment is the beachfront area known as the Stump Hole.*

The eastern elbow of Cape San Blas holds a curious phenomenon known by locals as the Stump Hole. Sand live oaks overtaken by the elements left behind roots and stumps that now pepper along the beaches and extend offshore for several hundred feet. The habitat lures a variety of species, as well as anglers hoping to fish amongst the picturesque.

Flounder and whiting are taken here using cut baits, such as squid, and live or freshly dead shrimp. A basic bottom rig positioned among the stumps draws flounder up to 2 pounds and whiting in the 12- to 15-inch range. Grubs jigged along the bottom are the best artificial lures for flounder. Jigs with bright yellows, reds, and pinks are another option.

Pompano, bluefish, and mackerel frequent here too. The best live baits include sand fleas and shrimp. Pink-and-white jigs ranging from $5/8$ to 1 ounce are effective artificials when retrieved swiftly. However, your best chance for hooking these latter species is to wade out and cast beyond the wave break. These fish travel close to shore from time to time but run more consistently beyond the first sand bar.

Spanish Mackerel: April to June—spoons
Flounder: October to March—live shrimp, grubs
Pompano: March through May, September to November—jigs
Bluefish: March to November—live bait, jigs
Whiting: March to November—cut bait

34) Grassy Flats

Directions: *From US 331, turn east onto US 98. Pass through Panama City into Port St. Joe. As you are leaving Port St. Joe, the St. Joseph Bay approaches US 98 to within 20 feet during high tide. At low tide the flats extend several hundred yards from the shore. Parking is abundant here on either side of the street.*

St. Joseph Bay provides some of the most phenomenal wade fishing in the region. At low tide the water recedes several hundred yards providing an excellent opportunity to scout for holes, sloughs, and other irregularities in the floor. Take the time to catch bait fish during low tide too. Finger mullet and bull minnows are easily netted after becoming trapped in the shallows by the swiftly receded waters.

At higher tides the water fluctuates between knee to waist deep, and the grass beds fill with speckled trout and redfish. Lures that dive when retrieved and live shrimp are the preferred baits. A moderately retrieved plug gives both species the opportunity to strike, and shrimp suspended 2 to 3 feet below the surface are an almost guaranteed success when fished near the water/grass line.

Wading farther offshore accesses different species. Bluefish, pompano, mackerel, among others, cruise throughout these flats in search of food. Finger mullet or jigs fished in the sloughs and depressions provide the desired results. A good technique is to cast a jig over a depression and retrieve across it. Fish hide along the edges of these holes waiting to ambush bait fish as they swim across. Remember to wear footwear whenever wade fishing. A number of man-made objects and underwater species, like stingrays, bite unsuspecting anglers from time to time.

> *Redfish: Spring, late September through November—*
> *alewives, blue crabs*
> *Speckled Trout: May, September through December—live*
> *shrimp, artificial lures*
> *White Trout: Spring, September through November—live*
> *shrimp*
> *Pompano: March through May, September to November—jigs*
> *Bluefish: March to November—live bait, jigs*

35) Low Docks

Directions: *From US 331 turn east onto US 98. Pass through Panama City, Mexico Beach, and over the two bridges leading into Port St. Joe. Cross over the railroad tracks and take a right onto First Street. The road dead-ends at a warehouse. Park here. When facing the water the Low Docks are down and to the left.*

In certain areas the St. Joseph Bay bottom was dragged to accommodate ocean-going vessels frequenting the nearby paper mill. The Low Docks provide fishermen access to one such spot where the deep waters can be angled without a boat. A concrete seawall runs along the Bay for several hundred feet, and the immediate waters are deep enough to support any species.

Crevalles and Spanish mackerel are common catches during their according seasons. On calm days, use a moderate retrieve with spoons and other shiny artificial lures. When the waters are rough, leading the lure with a float adds the surface disturbance necessary to get the fish's attention. Jigs tipped with cut bait are another proven artificial that attract the above mentioned and also draw bluefish and pompano. Cast straight out from the wall and jig the lure, stall for a half count, and jig again. Continue the process until another cast is necessary.

Fishing down this wall is an alternate technique. Groupers hole up at the base and in depressions along the seawall. Cut bait or shrimp fished on the bottom or suspended at various depths suffices in drawing them from these dens. Groupers fight hard, steady battles, but fishing them in this manner can be slow. I recommend setting out one line for this purpose and fishing a second line to work the other species.

Jack Crevalle: July and August—finger mullet, jigs
Bluefish: March to November—live bait, jigs
Sheepshead: February through March—live shrimp, sand
*   fleas*
Spanish Mackerel: April through May, September through
*   November—spoons*
Grouper: Spring, Fall—cut bait

36) Indian Pass

Directions: *From US 331 turn east onto US 98 and pass through Mexico Beach and Port St. Joe (making sure to stay on 98 after Port St. Joe). Follow the US 98 signs through downtown Apalachicola, cross over the bridge, then turn right onto Island Avenue (which turns into Franklin Boulevard), cross two more bridges onto St. George Island. The island has several boat launches for accessing the passes and bays in the area. Indian Pass is located at the western end of Apalachicola Bay.*

Fishing passes from a skiff or other watercraft is extremely prosperous along the Emerald Coast. Indian Pass is one of the best, though not the only. The following can be referenced when angling from a small vessel in any bay, sound, or outlet.

Fish merge when traveling narrow passes. This bottleneck effect concentrates more fish into a smaller area, thus increases the odds of drawing strikes. Hook live bait fish, like pinfish and mullet, at various points on their bodies (as discussed in the opening section), and experiment with depths. For red drum, position bait fish on the bottom with an upward swimming action. For members of the jack family, which cruise nearer the surface, rig a live bait through the lip and float it on the surface. Also, troll or drift the bait in the currents for an added advantage. Tarpon also show in decent numbers around passes, particularly Indian Pass. Retrieve large spoons or strip baits at a moderate to slow speed, but keep them off the bottom. Tarpon strike lures near the top while rolling along the surface to take in atmospheric oxygen. Oversized jigs, colored with yellows, pinks, and reds, work as all-around artificials. Tip them with cut bait to add scent.

Whenever possible, use live bait here, and stick with the theory that if you want to catch bigger fish, you need to use bigger bait. These channels produce large specimens alongside the smaller ones commonly caught from shore. Bullreds, black drums, tarpon, dolphin, and jacks can reach 10 to 100 pounds and more.

> *Tarpon: July through August—strip bait, shiny spoons*
> *Spanish Mackerel: April to June—spoons*
> *Pompano: March through May, September to November—jigs*
> *Bluefish: March to November—live bait, jigs*
> *Redfish: Spring, Fall—plugs, blue crabs*

37) West Point, St. George Island
Directions: *From US 331 turn east onto US 98 and pass through Mexico Beach and Port St. Joe (making sure to stay on 98 after Port St. Joe). Follow the US 98 signs through downtown Apalachicola, cross over the bridge, then turn right onto Island Avenue. Continue south onto St. George Island, then turn right onto the beachfront road.*

St. George Island's West Point is an excellent angling venue because it is not overcrowded. Unfortunately, the point is prohibited to the general public. Only residents or vacationers staying in the area known as the Plantation are allowed (unless special arrangements are made via local fishing guides). If you plan to vacation on St. George Island, rent a unit in the Plantation to avoid the hassles. The East Point is a better option for the one-day fisherman.

Here the competition is minimal and the waters teem with game fish. Redfish, sheepshead, flounder, pompano, and sharks are common catches. During season, pompano are the most sought-after quarry (see Hot Spot 39 for details). Live shrimp and sand fleas lure various species, including redfish, sheepshead, and flounder. Brightly colored grubs and jigs are suggested artificial lures. Tip them with cut bait to increase your odds. For sharks, bait with live pinfish and slice along the flanks to release blood and oils for scent. Vary the bait depth and chum with canned sardines if necessary. Most important-ly, know your tides. The tide frequency differs here from elsewhere on the Emerald Coast. (Remember, the best fishing is always during the onset of falling tides or the beginning of rising tides). Free tide tables are available at Survivors Island Bait and Tackle.

> *Sheepshead: February through March—live shrimp, sand*
> > *fleas*
> *Spanish Mackerel: April to June—spoons*
> *Flounder: October to March—live shrimp, grubs*
> *Pompano: March through May, September to November—jigs*
> *Bluefish: March to November—live bait, jigs*
> *Whiting: March to November—cut bait*
> *Redfish: Spring, Fall—plugs, blue crabs*

38) Bridge Island

Directions: *From US 331 turn east onto US 98 and pass through Mexico Beach and Port St. Joe (making sure to stay on 98 after Port St. Joe). Follow the US 98 signs through downtown Apalachicola, cross over the bridge, then turn right onto Island Avenue. Cross over the first bridge onto Bridge Island. Ample parking is available on both sides of the road.*

Bridge Island is fortified with a seawall providing an excellent platform for open-water and structure fishing in the Apalachicola Bay. Unfortunately, limited fishing locales around St. George Island causes congestion here. If possible, avoid the crowds by fishing the weekdays, especially outside the peak tourist season. If not, enough game fish are in this bay to go around.

Trout, mackerel, and flounder are common quarry caught from this seawall. Spoons lure the mackerel and occasionally draw members of the jack family. However, spoons often appear too sluggish for jacks. Switch to a swiftly retrieved jig with plenty of action when jacks move into the area. Live shrimp lure trout and flounder, and reign as the best all-around bait when you are unsure what is biting.

Sheepshead and redfish hang around the pilings. Sand fleas are prime bait for sheepshead. Bait the sand flea on a short shank hook and do not use a leader. Sheepshead are leery fish and any obtrusive terminal tackle reduces strikes. Drift a sand flea around the pilings (where this species forages barnacles), and experiment with various depths. For redfish, sink a shrimp to the bottom or use a float to keep it suspended about 1 foot off the floor. The currents provide the needed action. Re-bait with a fresh shrimp if nothing bites — scent is essential in luring these bottom dwellers. If shrimp fail altogether, 2- to 3-inch blue crabs (with their shells removed) are a proven alternative.

> **Flounder:** *October to December — cut bait*
> **Redfish:** *Spring, late September through November — alewives, blue crabs*
> **Sheepshead:** *February through March — live shrimp, sand fleas*
> **Spanish Mackerel:** *April through May, September through November — spoons*
> **Speckled Trout:** *May, September through December — live shrimp, alewives*

39) East Point, St. George Island
Directions: *From US 331 turn east onto US 98 and pass through Mexico Beach and Port St. Joe (making sure to stay on US 98 after Port St. Joe). Follow the US 98 signs through downtown Apalachicola, cross over the bridge, then turn right onto Island Avenue. Cross over the two bridges onto St. George Island and take a left where the road comes to a dead end.*

Fish migrating west in the springtime either run the pass between Dog Island and St. George Island or travel Gulf-side toward San Blas Bay. This split occurs at the eastern end of St. George Island, creating a premier angling spot along the Emerald Coast. However, a four-wheel-drive vehicle is necessary to reach the East Point. Visit Survivor's Island Bait & Tackle for information on renting vehicles or hiring tour guides.

A high concentration of fish inhabit these waters year-round, but no time is more prosperous than during the spring and fall pompano runs. Sand fleas, shrimp, and jigs are their preferred baits. Use pink-and-white or pink-and-yellow color schemes when fishing artificial lures, and do not use a leader. Terminal tackle must be kept minimal to catch pompano consistently. Usually a fast retrieve works best with a jig. However, pompano sometimes trail an artificial lure too far inshore before striking, thus get spooked by an unsightly angler. In this case, slow your retrieve, or fish a sand flea or shrimp in the sloughs instead.

Bluefish often run alongside pompano. If bluefish show, use a monofilament leader, around 12-pound test line, to inhibit their razor teeth. You will still lose the occasional rig to the bluefish, but anything heavier scares the pompano away.

Redfish, flounder, and sheepshead are resident species here. Bottom fishing live shrimp draws the redfish and flounder in their according seasons. In early springtime sheepshead strike shrimp too, but sand fleas prove more successful.

Spanish Mackerel: April to June—spoons
Flounder: October to March—live shrimp, grubs
Pompano: March through May, September to November—jigs
Sheepshead: February through March—live shrimp, sand
   fleas
Whiting: March to November—cut bait
Redfish: Spring, Fall—plugs, blue crabs

40) St. George Island Surfside

Directions: *From US 331 turn east onto US 98 and pass through Mexico Beach and Port St. Joe (making sure to stay on US 98 after Port St. Joe). Follow the US 98 signs through downtown Apalachicola, cross over the bridge, then turn right onto Island Avenue. Pass over two bridges onto St. George Island.*

Surf fishing is prime along any stretch of St. George Island coastline as long as you avoid crowds, watercrafts, and holiday weekends. Nothing ruins fishing like the constant commotion of swimmers and watercrafts. If happenstance has you vacationing during spring break, then fish the early mornings before the waters become crowded.

Fish migrating in spring arrive earlier here than those locales to the west, and specimens exceeding the normal size occur frequently. Pompano and bluefish are commonly caught. White jigs with pink or yellow tails lure them and also prove effective in hooking the occasional sheepshead. Fish with live shrimp between the first and second sand bars to locate these species with live baits. During autumn, spot fish for returning schools when the sun is near the eastern horizon. This low trajectory of light illuminates the waters without producing a glare and makes discerning the schools easier. Live shrimp also lure the resident bottom dwellers, like drums, flounder, and whiting. Fish them on a basic bottom rig in all but the hottest and coldest months.

Spanish Mackerel: *April to June—spoons*
Pompano: *March through May, September to November—jigs*
Bluefish: *March to November—live bait, jigs*
Whiting: *March to November—cut bait*
Redfish: *Spring, Fall—plugs, blue crabs*
Sheepshead: *February through March—live shrimp, sand fleas*

Fish Species, Habitats and Angling Techniques

The following list of fish species includes game fish and non-game fish privy to the Emerald Coast waters. Noted with each species are their habitats, proven angling techniques, and tips for identifying catches. Use this information to supplement the Hot Spots reference charts. Each species section concludes with an edibility rating. It is based on a 0-10 scale with 0 being the worst and 10 the best. Ratings were determined by personal preference, thus the scale is biased toward my favorites, the whiter-meat species. Always check with the local market if you have questions concerning the edibility of a fish. Some species contain parasites that can be harmful.

Barracuda

Description: Barracuda, or great barracuda as they are often called, have silver bodies with lighter bellies and varying dark blotches across their backs. Their bodies are long and sleek, coming to a point at the nose. Rose-colored teeth distinguish this hunter, which reaches weights of more than 100 pounds. The average size found in the northern Gulf of Mexico is 20 to 30 pounds.

Habitat: Smaller barracuda, in the 3- to 5-pound range, occasionally venture into the passes, bays, and sounds in the warmer months. During the warmest spells, barracuda are found in the shallow waters embroidering the banks, especially during high tides. They venture to the deeper canals and passes as the tide recedes. Also, barracuda are hooked off the end of piers from March to November but retreat from all inshore waters when the cold returns.

Angling Techniques: Catching these toothy creatures requires a wire leader. Eighteen- to 20-pound test braided wire is sufficient for all but the mightiest. The best live baits are mullet and eels. Live eels are usually not a viable option, but the synthetic versions are proven winners. Tipping the hook with a scented bait enhances your chances of luring them.

Another common way of hooking the barracuda occurs when you are reeling in another catch. The barracuda senses the fish struggling on the end of your line and seizes the opportunity. Sometimes they devour only the back half of the fish. Other times they take the entire fish and hook in the process.

Barracuda are strong swimmers and fighters and take baits with a vengeance. Play them long and hard, letting them take line when necessary and gaining ground only when they stall to regroup. This species is also a jumper. Many have leaped from the water into the boat in the final stages of a fight. This can prove to be a dangerous situation, so keep a good head when landing this fish. Also, barracuda are drawn to shiny objects, so do not use gold or silver terminal tackle, and keep jewelry, like rings, out of sight. Barracuda have been known to bite anglers, and spouses don't like their mates returning from fishing trips minus any digits.

Edibility, 0.

Black Drum

Description: Black drums have short, deep bodies, high-arching backs, and overbites. They are marked with faint dark and silver bands and blackish fins but are absent of the tail spot found on another drum, the redfish. Their most notable features are the barbels that look like chin whiskers. The average catch ranges from 10 to 40 pounds, but black drums are known to near the 150-pound mark.

Habitat: Black drums inhabit the sandy areas in lagoons and bays of the northern Gulf. Also, they are found in the surf, running bay passes, and in brackish lakes. This bottom dweller uses its chin barbels to locate mollusks and shellfish along the ocean floor. Although a resident fish, its numbers increase during the spring and fall migratory seasons.

Angling Techniques: Black drums are slow-striking, hard-fighting fish commonly caught off the bottom. Their teeth are located in the throat so a wire leader is not necessary. This species is an incidental catch rarely sought as a game fish. Black drum are usually hooked when fishing for redfish and speckled trout.

Edibility, 5 (when thoroughly cooked, as parasites can be a problem).

Black Grouper (Gag)

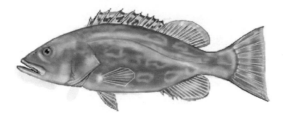

Description: Gag are a common grouper caught along the Emerald Coast. Their uniform gray coloration sets them apart from the other, more elaborate family species. They have an under-bite and grow to over 3 feet long. Some weigh more than 50 pounds. The mean size in the Gulf of Mexico is 2 to 3 pounds with a length of 15 to 20 inches.

Habitat: Gag are drawn to man-made structures, such as bridges, jetties, and walls. They inhabit dens provided by holes and indentations in these structures. Many are resident fish, meaning they do not migrate and can be found year-round. Usually gag are hooked incidentally while fishing for another species. However, after tremendous storms, like hurricanes, they arrive in large numbers inshore and take precedence on many anglers' hit lists.

Angling Techniques: A heavy monofilament is essential because gag live in dens. They take your bait, then dart for shelter. If they find shelter under the rocks or in the walls, heavy tension is essential to force them out. Tag about 10 yards of 40- to 60-pound test line onto your spooled line when fishing these den dwellers. This allows you the extra strength to pull them from the dens without snapping your line. Also, the line is less likely to break when it comes in contact with various structures.

Rig with an 8- to 10-ounce egg sinker about 18 inches up the leader. Bait with freshly dead shrimp or cut bait. Alewives and pinfish are good alternatives, and cobia jigs bounced along the bottom are also effective. (Do not add a sinker with the cobia jig.) Fish the deep waters, like harbor walls, by dropping the bait straight down the wall. Position the bait on the bottom or experiment with various depths along the wall to lure gag from their dens.

Edibility, 8.

Note: Jewfish, another type of grouper, are protected by law and must be released.

Black, Mangrove, and Vermilion Snappers

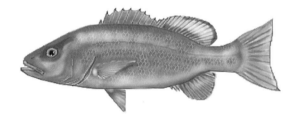

Description: Although several snapper species inhabit the Emerald Coast waters, black snappers are the most likely to venture inshore. Their dusky coloring accentuated with a mahogany undertone separates them from the other snapper species.

Mangrove and vermilion are two other species that are found in the northern Gulf of Mexico. Mangrove range from pale to dark and can be decorated with a variety of blotches and bars. Vermilion are red with white blotches. Common to all snappers are large eyes, diagonal foreheads, and slightly pouting under-bites. They reach lengths of 20 inches.

Habitat: Considered an offshore fish, snappers occasionally move inshore to feed around the piers, jetties, and bridges. During foul weather they seek shelter in the passes and bays.

Angling Techniques: Two fangs decorate a snapper's mouth, but a wire or monofilament leader is not necessary. A long shank hook provides enough protection to your line. Fishing from a dock or boat is successful when using shrimp without additional weight. Cast and let the bait drift slowly toward the bottom. Add a 12-inch, 15-pound monofilament leader if you continue to have your line clipped. Snappers are big market fish and have grown wise to man's intentions over the years. The extra tackle may be enough to scare them away.

Know where the snappers are running before seeking them. Many areas along the Gulf never house these species. Aside from the incidental catch, the Gulf Shores, Alabama, area is your best bet for landing a snapper.

Edibility, 8.

Bluefish

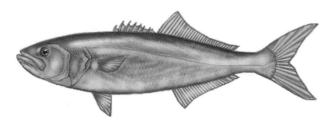

Description: Bluefish have an exaggerated under-bite, streamlined bodies, and prominent, dangerous teeth. Their bellies are silvery, and their backs are blue with darker blue fins. They can reach over 3 feet long from forked tail to head and weigh up to 50 pounds. In the northern Gulf they generally range from 3 to 8 pounds.

Habitat: Bluefish migrate in a more latitudinal orientation than other Gulf species. During the first warm days of March they begin moving west along the Panhandle and are often seen just outside the first sand bar, or near jetties and passes, thrashing the surface waters in a feeding frenzy. Bluefish move in large schools easily spotted from shore. Their frequency diminishes in the heat of summer, but they return from September through November as they migrate eastward. This end of summer run is the best time to angle bluefish.

Angling Techniques: Bluefish are a tenacious and exciting game fish along the Emerald Coast. They are extremely hard hitting and hard fighting and strike almost any bait, anywhere. Pompano jigs or cut bait provide excellent results. A wire leader is imperative due to their razor-sharp teeth. These canine teeth are extremely dangerous and have accounted for a number of attacks on swimmers and anglers over the years. Use extreme caution when landing bluefish, because they will attempt to bite as you remove the hook.

For casting at schools of bluefish, or any other schools, throw the lure several yards over and in front of the school. Begin reeling as soon as the bait hits the water, and retrieve swiftly with moderate action. As the bait passes in front of the school a few fish leave the school and tail it toward shore. The competition falls away and the last fish takes the bait. Catch several from one school by running ahead of them on the beach and waiting their arrival.

Edibility, 5.

Bonito (Little Tunny)

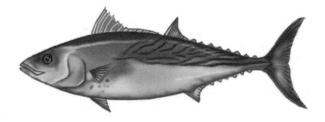

Description: Bonito have silver stomachs, shiny sides, and silvery blue backs. Their fins are grayish, and the upper portion of their flanks are striped from the gills to the tail. Some specimens develop yellow stripes during feeding times. The average bonito weighs 3 to 5 pounds and the largest reach 20 pounds. These larger fish may grow up to 3 feet long.

Habitat: Bonito usually travel in large schools. They inhabit bays, passes, and the waters off the ends of piers. The majority of their diet consists of alewives and mackerel, and they venture into high salinity waters in pursuit of them.

Angling Techniques: A little tunny is an extremely tenacious fish and excellent quarry to fight on light tackle. Baiting for them becomes a matter of what bait fish are prevalent in the area. Proven live baits along the northern Gulf include alewives and small ronkers. However, if finger mullet are in abundance, bait with them. Spoons and plastic squid are good artificial baits, and cut baits are not to be ruled out.

Bonito are a hard-hitting fish with a toothy mouth. A medium-weight wire leader is necessary. No hook set is necessary due to their vigor when taking the bait. They are sporadic fish that surge rapidly and turn without notice. The fight is as strong as any salt-water species. Release bonito upon landing unless you plan to use them as bait for later in the day. They are an extremely bloody fish, thus poor eating.

Edibility, 0.

Pompano Dolphin (Chicken Dolphin)

Description: Pompano dolphin have long been accused of being small dolphin fish (mahi-mahi). However, they are a separate species very similar in appearance to the female dolphin fish. They are characterized by their high, vertical foreheads, deep bodies through the chest region, and deeply forked tails. Their yellow bellies fade to green, then to deep blue along their backs and continuous dorsal fin. They reach lengths of around 2 ½ feet and weigh up to 7 pounds.

Habitat: Chicken dolphin, as they are most commonly referred to along the Emerald Coast, are found in the surf and bays during the summer months. In the Gulf they are accessible only from the ends of piers. Floating debris, like Styrofoam dislodged from docks, attracts them to the surface of bay waters.

Angling Techniques: Pompano dolphin strike hard and put up a mean fight. They are jerky and feisty and dive fast and return to the surface faster. Alewives hooked through the lip for a forward swimming motion are good bait for chicken dolphin. Do not add weight. This keeps the bait fish on the surface, where pompano dolphin are most likely to hit.

Silver spoons are excellent artificial lures when retrieved swiftly. Tipping the spoon's hook with strip bait for scent increases the effectiveness of the artificial lure. A pompano jig retrieved quickly enough to keep it near the surface draw strikes, too.

Edibility, 6.

Cobia (Ling, Lemon Fish)

Description: With an elongated body, under-bite, and long head, cobia are categorized as a species all their own. They have small teeth, a hard mouth, and are dark brown on top with beige sides and underbody. The fins are dark colored. A defining feature is the horizontal black band running from head to tail. In the Gulf of Mexico waters they range from 10 pounds to over 100 pounds. In recent years, many 50- to 100-pounders have been landed along the Emerald Coast.

Habitat: Cobia begin migrating from west to east in mid-March and continue through mid-May. During this period they are close enough to shoreline to catch from a pier. In the Gulf waters they move along or just outside the second sand bar alone or in pairs or pods. At times they venture to slightly greater depths. Other times they come close enough to be spotted in the belly of a breaking wave.

Angling Techniques: Usually cobia are caught while spotting from boats with towers, but many are hooked from the piers and surf in the high season. In recent years large cobia have returned to the Emerald Coast. Countless tournaments cater to this fish in the springtime, and record-breaking catches occur monthly.

Generally the barefoot fisherman does not venture out specifically for this fish. Carry an extra rig in case one is spotted while seeking other game fish. Casting all day for these beasts is overbearing. Throwing at the occasional drifter is the way to go. Oversized jigs, or boathead lures, tipped with cut bait are commonly used. Occasionally a large minnow-shaped lure works to attract them. Effective live baits include 6- to 8-inch mullet and blue crabs about 5 inches in length.

Edibility, 8.

Florida Pompano

Description: Also referred to as pompano, a stubby, deep body characterizes this species. Their upper portion is bluish-gray with silvery sides, and the fins and underbelly are yellowish. Florida pompano are soft mouthed with no dangerous teeth, and often are mistaken for their larger cousins, permit. An average size is 2 to 3 pounds, although at times 4- to 5-pounders are not uncommon.

Habitat: Florida pompano are resident fish in certain depressions along the Emerald Coast shores. Other schools migrate through the area just outside the first sand bar, greatly increasing the springtime numbers. Autumn is good for catching pompano, too, as they migrate toward the warmer waters farther south. Mostly a surf fish, they are found around jetties, piers, and other structures, and occasionally in inland waters with a high saltwater influence.

Angling Techniques: Pompano are a notoriously frantic species. They strike hard and fast and run with bait for great distances before the fight begins. Let them play themselves out on a long line, and keep constant tension against them. Land pompano only after their frenzy-like behavior is over.

Pompano hunt more by sight than smell, and too much terminal tackle spooks them. No leader is required due to their soft mouths, although they often run alongside bluefish and other toothy creatures that will clip your line. When this problem arises use a monofilament leader, around 20-pound test, tagged directly to the reel line (no swivel). This keeps unsightly terminal tackle minimal. The best surf fishing baits are sand fleas or 5/8-ounce pompano jigs with red-and-white heads and pinkish skirts. Use a fast retrieve with artificial lures. Live shrimp and sand fleas are other prime targets for these hunters. Position them on the bottom or allow them to drift in the mid-waters.

Edibility, 9.

Gulf Flounder

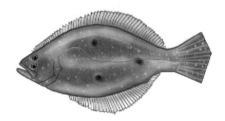

Description: These flat fish are light brown on the top side with dusky blotches. As with most flat fish, both eyes move to a single side of the body, in this case the left side. The left side becomes their upward orientation at a young age. Their blind side, or the side that moves along the ocean floor, is white or very lightly pigmented. Gulf flounder are a relatively small species of flat fish, ranging from 10 to 15 inches along the Emerald Coast.

Habitat: Flounder are bottom-dwelling fish found over inshore sands, deeper waters, and in the bays and lagoons. From March to late November they inhabit the surf waters, camouflaging themselves by lying atop, or just underneath, the sand. During these same months they are found in abundance in bays and lagoons and are best hunted at night.

Angling Techniques: Bouncing a grub or jig along the bottom with a slow retrieve is an excellent method for fishing flounder in the surf. They follow the lure almost to the beach before striking.

Watch them approach behind the lure, then stall it near shore to provide them the chance to strike. Flounder also attack bottom rigs baited with cut bait or freshly dead shrimp. Good live baits include minnows, alewives, and shrimp baited on a sliding sinker rig. Position these baits on or near the bottom.

Gigging is another popular method for catching flounder. With the proper equipment, catching the limit is common during this unique fishing experience. See the previous section on gigging for more information.

Edibility, 8.

Hardtail (Blue Runner)

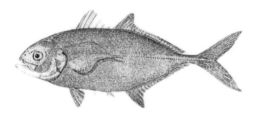

Description: Hardtails are members of the jack family, although their bodies are more slender than other jacks. They have deeply forked tails and sharp teeth. Their backs are a bluish-green with darker green fins, and their chests yellow to silver. Some reach lengths of 30 inches, but the average specimen is around 1 foot.

Habitat: Mostly an offshore fish, hardtails sporadically come to inshore waters and through the passes into the bays. They are somewhat migratory, traveling north and west along the Emerald Coast in the springtime and south and east in the autumn.

Angling Techniques: Most commonly blue runners are used as live bait for larger game fish. They are hooked while casting, trolling, and still-fishing. Use a rig with an egg weight for bottom fishing or a quickly retrieved jig when working an artificial lure. Bait with shrimp, jigs, or spoons. Keep your eyes on the water when blue runners are present. They often draw larger game fish to the area.

Cutting the tail and bleeding them upon catching will provide a much more appetizing entree.

Edibility, 7.

Jack Crevalle (Crevalle Jack)

Description: Jack crevalle are bluish-green on top and pale yellow below with a forked tail. They are characterized by a blunt nose, slight under-bite, and forward eyes. The largest of the species reach 50 pounds, although 2- to 4-pounders are most commonly pulled from running schools.

Habitat: Crevalle jacks of all sizes are found cruising inshore waters. They are voracious eaters and often school in flats near shorelines. The larger specimens move in pairs or pods and chase bait fish up to the shoreline. Also, crevalles are spotted rounding up bait fish, such as mullet, for feeding just offshore. Look for white water or an oily film at the Gulf surface. Gulls circling overhead is another good sign.

Angling Techniques: Jack crevalles are some of the fiercest game fish. They require a speedily retrieved lure. Slow retrieves are neglected by crevalles. They have a tough mouth, thus a quick retrieve prevents the regurgitating of the hook and also helps set it. They rap the lure quickly and fight to the finish, often threatening with a final surge before being landed. Setting the hook is not necessary because of their quick, hard hit.

They are toothy critters, so use a leader. A monofilament between 25- to 40-pound test is sufficient. Artificial lures that can be retrieved swiftly, such as pompano jigs and Mirrolures, are effective. Lip-hook live bait fish and either float them on the surface or add weight to position them in the mid-waters. Mullet, pinfish, and ronkers are the preferred live baits.

Edibility, 5 (under 18 inches), 2 (over 18 inches).

Ladyfish (Tenpounder)

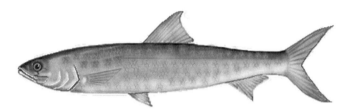

Description: Ladyfish have slender bodies with predominately silver bellies and sides, bluish-green backs, and darker tails. Their eyes are forward and oversized. The tenpounder name is misleading because they rarely achieve weights of more than 6 pounds. They are quite large, however, with lengths of up to 3 feet. As a close relative of the tarpon, the false name derives from their incredible fighting ability.

Habitat: Ladyfish usually inhabit the shallows of bays and estuaries, hovering near or over the sandy and muddy clearings. At times they travel in large schools running the shoreline and in and out of the passes. The schools are frequently spotted around bridge pilings when they are in bays.

Ladyfish behave like bluefish when seen in the surf. During the summer months they school along the coastline creating a surface-water frenzy as they feed. Their magic water temperature is 76 degrees, which brings them to the northern Gulf in June and leads them away in September.

Angling Techniques: Ladyfish are strong fighters like their cousins, bonefish. They tend to ignore slow prey, thus respond best to rapidly retrieved lures. Gold and silver spoons, pompano jigs, and other artificial lures that shine are the best bet.

The tenpounder is a spectacular catch. They thrash wildly when taking surface lures and leap throughout the fight. Use a light wire leader, not because of sharp teeth or mouth, but because their bodies are extremely abrasive and likely to snap a monofilament leader during a fight.

Edibility, 0.

King Mackerel

Description: King mackerel, or kings, are one of the largest species in the mackerel family, reaching up to 100 pounds and 5 feet in length. The body is elongated with grayish-green on the back and silver on the sides and belly. They have forked tails and sharp teeth. Most king mackerel are striped rather than spotted like their close cousins, the Spanish mackerel. However, the younger species do occasionally have spots, making it difficult to differentiate the two.

Habitat: Kings run offshore in schools and are a popular fish for offshore trolling. In early May, however, they come close enough inshore to catch from piers. They stay throughout the summer and into the fall until the water temperature drops below 72 degrees, usually in early November. During this period they close to within 150 yards off the coastline.

Angling Techniques: King mackerel in the 40- to 50-pound class are not uncommon along the Emerald Coast. The first time you hook a species of this size and power changes your perspective on fishing. The most exciting way to fish kings is to free-line. To free-line, cast a live bait fish off the end of a pier and let it struggle across the surface waters. Leave the reel bail open so the bait fish can take out line. The line then peels easily when a king strikes. Keep the drag light at first and slowly increase as necessary—making sure to stop before the line snaps. Good artificial baits are large Rapalas that make noise and stir the surface for top-water feeding.

King mackerel run at 40 miles per hour after taking a bait. No hook set necessary. Let a king take the line without a fight on its initial run. The line will pop if you try to fight it at this point. Kings slow after taking several hundred yards of line. Now is the time to start working the fish. Let kings take line when necessary, and pump the reel and gain ground only when the fish is not surging. Large kings make several long runs before tiring.

Edibility, 7.

Mullet

Description: The Gulf of Mexico is privy to many mullet species. Most commonly seen are striped mullet. Fatbacks, or jumpers, as they are sometimes called, are predominately silver with some bluish-green. The latter name evolves from their leaping style. They shoot nose first out of the water and reenter tail or belly first. The largest reach lengths of around 18 inches.

Habitat: Mullet inhabit the surf, bays, lagoons, and canals. During early morning and late evening they like to leap in the still waters. Along the Emerald Coast they travel in large schools, often succumbing to feasting game fish just outside the first sand bar.

Mullet are perhaps the most famed fish along the Emerald Coast. Several festivals drawing over fifty thousand people annually are dedicated to the fatback and its precarious nature. Author Michael Swindle delves into all the magic, mania, and lore surrounding this jumper in *Mulletheads,* a book that includes in-depth coverage of the mullet toss, a sport in a class all its own.

Angling Techniques: Mullet are herbivorous by nature and are rarely caught using lures or live bait. Occasionally they are hooked using dough balls or corn, and snagging one from a school with a hook is not uncommon. However, the best method for catching mullet is cast netting. The method is discussed in the previous section on using a cast net.

Edibility, 8.

Redfish (Red Drum, Channel Bass)

Description: Redfish are copper in color, with a black spot at the base of the tail. They have strong jaws and a noticeable under-bite but lack the chin barbels of black drums. They sometimes exceed 90 pounds (5 feet), but most mature adults, also know as bullreds, are around 40 pounds. The masses run less than 10 pounds.

Note: Some redfish may have two or three black spots. Others may have none. Usually these have been bred and released to help populate the waters.

Habitat: Redfish are a major game fish of the region, prominent year-round in the northern portion of the Gulf of Mexico. Some move from bay to bay. Others migrate in schools along the coastline, enhancing the population during their spring and fall runs. These bottom dwellers are particularly fond of the passes and grass beds but can be fished in all Emerald Coast waters.

Angling Techniques: The best period for catching redfish is in the fall from September throughout November. Their numbers are highest at this time, although they can be caught year-round. Bait live shrimp over a long shank hook. Add weight to the line to keep the rig near the bottom when fishing the passes and other deeper waters. Weight is not necessary when fishing along the grass beds, as shrimp sink in these temperate currents. Three- to 4-inch blue crabs and alewives are good live baits too.

Mirrolure- and Rapala-brand artificial lures attract redfish. Fish these along grass beds. A slow to moderate retrieve is recommended. Once hooked, redfish are notorious for long, deep dives. They fight a hard, steady battle and surge aggressively. Landing bullreds can take hours, making them a favorite of anglers along the Emerald Coast.

Edibility: 6 (under 15 pounds), 2 (over 15 pounds).

Ronker (Atlantic Croaker)

Description: Ronkers are a plentiful member of the drum family in the Gulf of Mexico. Most specimens are grayish along their backs, brownish-blue across their bellies, and have yellowish spots or lines decorating their flanks. The largest reach 2 feet in length, but most catches are half that size.

Habitat: Ronkers forage along the sandy bottoms of lakes, bays, and surf. They feed upon crustaceans, mollusks, and other creatures inhabiting the ocean floor. Their name derives from a grunting sound.

Angling Techniques: Croakers are not sought as game fish, although they are caught quite frequently when fishing other species. They are primarily a commercial fish harvested in great numbers. Smaller specimens are corralled in cast nets and used by anglers for live bait.

Edibility, 5.

Sailcat (Sloop Rig, Gafftopsail Catfish)

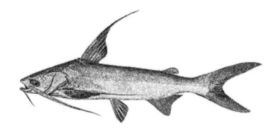

Description: Sailcats, as they are called along the Emerald Coast, are robust and wide-bodied fish with bluish-gray backs and lighter bellies. The elongated filament extending from the dorsal fin characterizes the sailcat, as do the whiskers common to all species of catfish. Common specimens are 6 inches to 2 feet in length and weigh up to 5 pounds.

Habitat: Sailcats frequently inhabit the deeper waters between the first and second sand bars. They are also prominent bottom dwellers in bays and lagoons during the spring and fall. Sailcats are

resident fish. Their numbers, however, decline during the hottest
and coldest months.

Angling Techniques: Sailcats are tough fighters pound for pound
but not sought as a game fish. They strike cut baits and shrimp
positioned on the bottom with a basic bottom rig. Alewives are
their preferred live bait. Occasionally they pursue a jig or other artificial lure, but natural baits are preferred.

Most anglers consider these catfish a nuisance and a disappoint-
ment when hooked. However, hooking them is relatively easy and
playing them is challenging.

Edibility, 5.

Sharks

Description: Many species of shark exist. In fact, there are over 250
types of sharks, ranging from 2 feet to 60 feet in length, and some
of them are considered game fish. As a general characterization,
sharks have a fusiform shape and cartilaginous frame. They have
skin, rather than scales, and most have rows of sharp teeth and a
nose that projects well beyond the mouth.

Habitat: Sharks are migratory, and many stay in constant motion to
meet their oxygen intake needs. They cruise at all water depths, and
some large species are frequently sighted along sand bars or bay
shallows. They inhabit most salt water worldwide.

Angling Techniques: Sharks can be hooked along the Emerald Coast in bays and surf, and from piers and boats. However, thoroughly research the topic or hire a guide if you are inexperienced. Landing sharks can be dangerous without the proper instruction. Often times the tail, rather than the teeth, bites an unsuspecting angler. Inexperienced anglers should cut the line rather than attempt to land a shark hooked incidentally.

Each shark species has its own flavor. Consult a fish market when a question about specific catches arise.

Edibility, 0-10.

Sheepshead

Description: Sheepshead have dark and light vertical stripes all along the body and are often referred to as convict fish. They have tall, compressed torsos, dark tails and heads, and incisor teeth for scraping barnacles. They reach 3 feet in length, but generally range from 1 to 2 feet.

Habitat: Sheepshead are prevalent year-round in the Gulf of Mexico. Their diet consists of barnacles, shellfish, and mollusks, so they are often found along pilings and rocks searching for food. Occasionally sheepshead inhabit the surf, but the smaller specimens linger in the bays around natural and man-made reefs.

Angling Techniques: Sheepshead are a most challenging opponent for the sports fisherman. They are an extremely suspicious fish with very particular appetites. Chumming with crustaceans is a proven method. Chum the water around pilings or other underwater structures until the water is cloudy. Once the sheepshead are drawn to the area, they feed and become confident with the chum. Bait a sand flea or fiddler crab on a short shank hook and dangle it amidst the chum cloud. The cloud helps the bait blend in so sheepshead will strike. Scraping barnacles off pilings also produces a similar clouding effect.

When not chumming, thread shrimp over a long shank hook or bait with a sand flea. Position the baits at various depths directly alongside pilings and underwater structures. Keep in mind that patience and persistence are the only consistent methods for landing this leery fish. Use a hard hook set and constant tension. Sheepshead play modestly on light or medium tackle.

Sheepshead have tough skins. Rather than spending hours scaling one, simply fillet the flank and bake them with their scales. When ready, the meat can be eaten directly from the skin.

Edibility, 7.

Southern Stingray

Description: Southern stingrays are discernible from most aquatic species by their discus-shaped bodies and whip-like tails. Their bodies are dark gray to dark brown, with darker wing edges. Their bottom sides are lightly pigmented. The largest specimens reach widths of 5 feet and lengths of 7 feet.

Habitat: These inshore fish forage for clams and shrimp in the surf and bay shallows, often skirting along the shoreline. They are well-known for burrowing below the sand or mud, and are responsible for the large, circular depressions left in their absence. At times stingrays cruise the surf coastline in schools.

Do not mistake southern stingrays with a similar looking species, the mantaray. Mantarays also school along the coastline and are often seen jumping vertically out of the water. However, this latter is a herbivorous species, thus will not strike a typical bait.

Angling Techniques: Although rarely an angler's choice bounty, these oddities are hooked while fishing for other species. Handling them with care is imperative due to possible wounds inflicted by the dangerous tail spine. Take precaution when wading in bays. The name stingray derives from the sensation created as this spine pierces the skin, and stingrays leave only their eyes and tail spine showing once burrowed into the sand or mud. Cut the line when large specimens are hooked to ensure a safe release for you. The hook will rust quickly out of the fish's mouth.

Edibility, 0.

Spadefish

Description: Spadefish are short and narrow and almost as tall as they are long. Most are grayish with four to six darker vertical bars. Some are more yellowish or greenish. The largest reach 3 feet and

20 pounds, but the average specimen is about one-third that length and weighs about 3 pounds.

Habitat: Spadefish move to the inland Gulf waters in the summer to feed on crustaceans. They forage around wrecks, sunken debris, and jetties in water with a high salt content. In autumn spadefish move into the surf and gather in large schools along the coastline before departing to deeper waters.

Angling Techniques: Spadefish are fished using fiddler crabs and sand fleas. Bait a short shank hook, cast, and keep the reel bail open. Let the bait drift slowly to the bottom, then retrieve, and repeat the process. Bottom rigs catch spadefish too. Fasten a bottom rig using 15- to 20-pound monofilament and an egg sinker. Bait with sand fleas, fiddler crabs, cut baits, or shrimp. Whipping your rod-tip adds action to a cut bait positioned on the bottom. Spadefish are moderate fighters, using their wide bodies to swim sideways against the pull of the rod.

Edibility, 8.

Spanish Mackerel

Description: Spanish mackerel have orange spots instead of stripes, like the king mackerel. They are deep blue on top with a pinkish-silver underside and blue fins. They have a slight overbite and a row of sharp teeth. Some reach 20 pounds, but 10 pounds is a large catch. One- to 3-pounders are common.

Habitat: Spanish mackerel begin running along the Emerald Coast in late March or early April, die out in the heat of summer, and return September through November. When running they are prevalent in passes, bays, and along the coastline.

Angling Techniques: Spanish mackerel have sharp teeth and must be fished with a wire leader. Use wire in the 18-pound range. Lusterless swivels are necessary. Spanish mackerel strike shiny tackle and clip the line. Jigs, feather lures, and spoons are effective artificial lures. Use a moderate retrieve and stall occasionally. When angling dirty or rough waters, create surface noise by using a popping artificial lure, or lead the bait with a float to help the fish locate the bait.

Live shrimp or cut bait are preferred natural baits. Suspend these in the mid-waters by attaching a float to the line at various distances from the hook. Experiment with the depth, but remember, once you find where they are hitting, stick with it until their feeding time is over. Finger mullet and alewives in the 3- to 4-inch range are good bait fish.

Spanish mackerel strike quickly and firmly, leaving little need to set the hook. They make numerous short runs, often becoming airborne before attempting to dive to deeper waters. They fight to the finish and usually make a final surge before being landed.

Edibility, 7.

Speckled Trout

Description: Speckled trout, or spotted seatrout or specks, are dark gray on top with a silver underside. Numerous spots decorate the species from head to tail, and the elders are likely to have spots on their yellowish-green fins. Their bodies are slender and elongated, tapering to pointed noses. Specks have soft mouths and two dominate front teeth. They generally range from 2 to 4 pounds, although specimens reaching 15 pounds or more have been landed.

Habitat: Speckled trout are a dominant game fish in the Emerald Coast region. They spawn in the bays and lagoons where the young remain throughout winter. Grass beds provide the young with protection and small crustaceans for food. The larger species move into the surf during the cold months but return to the inland waters in early spring. Speckled trout are a resident species along the Emerald Coast, but certain times of year are better than others for catching them.

Angling Techniques: Specks are an extremely popular game fish and are often angled alongside redfish. They are caught year round along the Emerald Coast in the bays and lagoons, and from the surf during the colder months. Speckled trout fluctuate their depth depending on time of day and water temperature. Experiment with a variety of depths and rigs to locate them.

Rigs for speckled trout vary greatly, but no wire leader is necessary, despite the two front teeth. Rig with monofilament leaders of

15 to 20 pounds. Anything more spooks these fish. Good bait fish include pinfish, alewives, and finger mullets. Lip-hook them, and lock the bail to keep the bait fish near the surface or leave it open to allow the bait fish to dive. Another proven technique is to suspend a shrimp in the mid-waters by using a float. Place a float above a 24-inch leader, and bait the shrimp over a long shank hook. Position the rig over the bald spots between grass beds. Proven artificial lures include top-water floaters, Mirrolures, and Rapalas.

A hook set is necessary with these fish, but their soft mouths require a fine touch. A medium tug is sufficient. Yanking too hard rips the mouth and frees the hook. Speckled trout are moderate fighters, and landing a large one with light tackle is quite a challenge.

Like all trout, specks are notoriously weak fish. Take extra care to ensure they do not die in the unhooking and releasing process. Handle them with a damp towel or damp cotton gloves. Keep their out-of-water time minimal to increase their chance of survival. Also, reviving the fish may be necessary. (See the section on releasing.)

Edibility, 10 (but they spoil quickly so should be iced ASAP).

Note: Another trout species along the Emerald Coast is the white trout. Smaller than the speck, white trout range from 1 to 3 pounds and have purplish backs and silverish bellies. They are found year-round in the bays and surf and are fished in the same manner as specks.

Tarpon

Description: Tarpon are easily discerned by their shiny silver sides and belly, and dark blue dorsal area. Often they are spotted rolling on the water surface as they take in extra oxygen from the atmosphere. Tarpon have an enormous under-bite, lean bodies, and reach weights around 300 pounds. Northern Gulf species generally range between 20 to 100 pounds.

Habitat: Usually considered a species of more southern regions, tarpon are also found in the northern waters of the Gulf of Mexico. They arrive to the shallower Emerald Coast waters with the warm temperatures of summer. Inshore brackish waters, bayous, and lagoons are favorite saltwater arenas for the tarpon farther south. But along the Gulf Coast they are best angled as they run through the passes. Tarpon also travel about 200 yards off the coastline, and are fished from the ends of piers. These game fish disappear as fall returns and the water temperatures drop.

Angling Techniques: Tarpon are called the silver kings of the game fish. They run with a bait for several hundred yards before engaging in battles that can last for hours on end. They are huge jumpers, fast swimmers, and among the most ferocious fighters.

Fishing these giants is tricky due to their light strike. Attempting to set the hook too soon results in yanking the lure from their mouth. A momentary pause after feeling the initial bump allows the fish to swallow, whereupon a hard yank or series of yanks sinks the hook into their tough jaws. Blue crabs 3 to 4 inches in length, alewives, and pinfish are the recommended live baits.

Lures that flash and shine are the best artificial lures. Rattle-traps, spoons, and Mirrolures are among this group.

Make sure tarpon are played out before attempting a landing. Many fishermen have died while landing tarpon prematurely. Once played out, lip-gaff them, and remove the hook with pliers or by pulling the bend out of the hook. Always release tarpon. Although edible, the taste is very poor.

Edibility, 1.

Tripletail

Description: The name tripletail derives from the swept-back dorsal and anal fins that create the illusion of this species having three tails. Their coloring is dark brown to brownish-yellow with blotches of lighter brown areas. They have deep bodies, sharp teeth, and reach lengths of around 3 ½ feet and weights of 50 pounds.

Habitat: Tripletail hang around buoys, channel markers, and underwater debris in the bays, sounds, and estuaries. Most commonly they are seen floating at the surface on their sides, an action that, with their coloration, helps disguise them as floating autumn leaves.

Angling Techniques: Tripletail are not sought after by most anglers, but incidental catches occur from time to time. The species is commonly caught around piers, pilings, and underwater structures. They put up a strong fight and are hooked while bottom fishing with live baits, like fiddler crabs or shrimp.

Edibility, 7.

Whiting

Description: Whiting are silvery white from tail to head with a single barbel on the chin. Some have hints of beige along their flanks. They rarely exceed a length of 12 inches.

Habitat: Whiting inhabit the sandy ocean floors along the coastline and occasionally venture into the bays. As bottom dwellers they feed predominantly on crabs and mollusks before proceeding to deeper waters in the coldest months. Whiting show in great numbers along the Emerald Coast from March through November.

Angling Techniques: Whiting are hooked consistently from the surf. Bait a surf fishing rig with cut bait, squid, or shrimp. Use a pyramid sinker to prevent the rig from being dragged by the currents. No leader is necessary. Position the bait just beyond the wave break.

Edibility, 7.

Local Recipes

No fishing guide is complete without a few suggestions on how to cook the catch. The following recipes highlight the flavor of the local catches, as well as the flavor of the local folk kind enough to pass them along.

BAKED REDFISH

3 tsp. butter
Juice from 1 lemon
1 clove garlic, crushed
4 redfish fillets, about 10 ounces each
1 tsp. dry white wine
Parmesan cheese

Preheat the oven at 325 degrees.

Melt butter, lemon juice, and crushed garlic. Baste the fillets lightly with this butter sauce.

Bake fillets for 10 minutes, remove from the oven, and baste again. Return the fish to the oven and bake for an additional 10 minutes. Remove the fish from the oven and sprinkle each fillet with 1 teaspoon of dry white wine.

Sprinkle with parmesan cheese. Serve with angel-hair pasta, using the remaining butter sauce on the noodles.

WHITEFISH CHOWDER

2 cups water
1 clove garlic, finely chopped
1 onion, chopped
$^1/_2$ cup sliced okra
$^1/_2$ cup red table wine
$^1/_2$ cup olive oil
3 tomatoes, diced
1 tsp. seasoned salt
2 stalks celery, chopped
$^1/_4$ tsp. white pepper
$^1/_2$ pound white-meat fish (pompano, flounder, whiting, etc.)

Heat the water to 350 degrees on a stovetop. Stir in the garlic, onion, and okra and cook for 5 to 7 minutes. Add the remaining ingredients, excluding the fish, and simmer for 20 minutes.

Cut the fish into $^1/_2$-inch cubes. Add the fish to the stock and simmer until cooked. Final simmering time varies according to fish variety chosen.

Best served with French bread and Greek-style salad.

GRILLED POMPANO

1 sheet aluminum foil
4 pompano fillets, about 10 ounces each
Juice from $^1/_2$ lemon
Italian dressing to taste
Black pepper to taste
White wine (optional)

Preheat grill to medium heat. Make a tray with the aluminum foil so that the sides turn up to retain the juices. Place the fish on the aluminum foil. Sprinkle the lemon juice over the fish. Baste with Italian dressing and dust with black pepper. This fish cooks quickly so turn accordingly. Add more lemon juice or a dash of white wine when cooking is completed to keep the meat moist.

Serve over wild rice with corn on the cob.

BLACKENED TROUT

4 Tbl. olive oil
$^1/_4$ clove garlic, finely chopped
4 speckled or white trout flanks with skin on one side,
about 8 ounces each
2 Tbl. blackened seasoning

For the best flavor, place a frying pan over an outside grill (although a stovetop can be used) at medium heat. Add olive oil to the pan, allow to heat, then dust with garlic.

Place the trout fillets skin-side down. Cook for 3 to 5 minutes. Turn once and cook for 2 minutes, then turn back to the skin side and add blackened seasoning. Grill skin-side down for another 1 to 2 minutes.

Serve with white rice and iceberg-lettuce salad. Eat trout carefully out of the skin, making sure to avoid the fine bones.

WHOLLY MACKEREL

3 mushrooms, thinly sliced
2 banana peppers, thinly sliced
1 tomato, thinly sliced
4 Tbl. vegetable oil
4 Spanish mackerel fillets, about 10 ounces each
8 Tbl. dry white wine
1 tsp. salt
1 Tbl. black pepper

Heat stovetop to 300 degrees. Stir-fry the mushrooms, banana peppers, and tomato in vegetable oil until soft.

Spread the vegetables on a baking sheet, then place the fillets over the vegetables. Sprinkle with salt and pepper. Turn up the heat and bake for approximately 20 minutes at 350 degrees. Splash about 2 tablespoons of white wine over the fillets every 5 minutes to keep them moist.

Serve as is or over a bed of white rice.

FRIED MULLET

4 cups vegetable oil
4 mullet fillets, about 8 ounces each, cut into strips or cubes
$1/4$ cup dried potato flakes
$1/2$ cup cornmeal
$1/4$ cup flour
3 tsp. seafood seasoning
1 tsp. salt
1 Tbl. black pepper
1 tsp. cayenne pepper
1 tsp. garlic powder
1 cup milk

Heat vegetable oil in a deep-fryer.

Mix dried potato flakes, cornmeal, and flour. Add seafood seasoning, salt, black pepper, cayenne pepper, and garlic powder. Pour this breading mix into a paper bag. Dunk the fish strips in milk, then coat with breading by placing them in a bag and shaking until thoroughly covered. Submerge them in the hot vegetable oil and allow to fry until the breading turns golden. Remove, drain, and allow to cool.

Delicious served with jalapeño hushpuppies and cheese grits.

BAKED POMPANO

4 pompano fillets, 8 to 10 ounces
2 lemons, sliced
1 tsp. lemon pepper
3 Tbl. butter, melted
$1/2$ tsp. salt

Preheat oven to 350 degrees. Slice three slits down each fillet and squeeze lemon juice into slits. Place fillets on a baking pan. Dust with lemon pepper and cover with butter. Place two or three lemon slices on each fillet. Bake for approximately 20 minutes. Remove from the oven and salt lightly.

Serve with cornbread dressing and salad.

Fishing Links

WEBSITES, ADDRESSES, AND TELEPHONE NUMBERS

To report emergencies or Florida saltwater fishing law violations: 800/342-5367 or dial *FMP on a cellular phone.

Alabama Marine Resources: (334) 861-2882

Gulf Telephone Fishline: 334/970-FISH
4 digit codes: 1131 Deep Sea Fishing Report
1132 Charter Boat Rental
1134 What Can I Expect to Catch Now

Walton County Artificial Reef Program
Pompano Consulting Engineering, Inc.
Van R. Butler III, P.E.
99 Hotz Avenue
Grayton Beach, FL 32459
Further information: 850/231-0982 or fax: 850/231-0981

Fishing Lines: A Quarterly Newsletter from the Division of Marine
Resources, Florida Department of Environmental Protection.
For further information contact:

Florida Department of Environmental Protection
Division of Marine Resources
Mail Station 240
3900 Commonwealth Boulevard
Tallahassee, FL 32399-3000
www.dep.state.fl.us

TACKLE SHOPS

Fort Walton Beach, Florida:

Pat's Bait and Tackle
293 Brooks Street SE
Fort Walton Beach, FL
850/244-5440

Gulf Breeze, Florida:

Gulf Breeze Bait and Tackle
825 Gulf Breeze Parkway
Gulf Breeze, FL 32561
850/932-6789

Orange Beach, Alabama:

J & M Tackle
25125 Canal Road
Orange Beach, AL 36561
334/981-5460
Fax: 334/981-5515

Panama City, Florida:

Half Hitch Tackle Co., Inc.
2206 Thomas Drive
Panama City Beach, FL 32408
850/837-3121
Fax: 850/837-4979
www.halfhitch.com

Port St. Joe, Florida:

Roy's Hardware, Bait & Tackle
306 Reid Avenue
Port St. Joe, FL 32456
850/229-8933

Presnell's Bayside Marina & R.V. Resort
Route 1, Box 109
Highway C-30
Port St. Joe, FL 32456
850/229-2710

St. George Island, Florida:

Survivors Island Bait and Tackle
28 West Pine Street
St. George Island, FL 32328
850/927-3113
www.homtown.com.survivors

SELECTED FISHING CHARTERS

Harborwalk Charters
P.O. Box 753
Destin, FL 32540
For reservations call 850/837-2343 or 800/242-2824

Captain Anderson's Marina Fishing Charter
Panama City Beach, FL
800/874-2415

Index to Fish Species